A VARIED HARVEST

A VARIED HARVEST

Out of a Teacher's Life and Thought

A Collection of Essays by

Frank E. Gaebelein

Headmaster Emeritus
Stony Brook School

This special edition
prepared for
THE AMERICAN TRACT SOCIETY
Oradell, N.J.

WILLIAM B. EERDMANS PUBLISHING COMPANY
Grand Rapids, Michigan

Preface

What one believes and what one does affect what he writes — a principle to which the essays in this book bear witness. They are the outcome of speaking in churches, educational institutions, and other places; many of them reflect years of teaching as well as recent editorial work; all of them relate in one way or another to the evangelical faith to which I am committed.

Service as co-editor of *Christianity Today* following long experience in writing has shown me how demanding the responsibility for the printed word can be. And even more demanding is a headmaster's responsibility for his students, as my forty-one years at The Stony Brook School have taught me. In either case, truth is the criterion for thought and action. Christ, the incarnate Word of God, is indeed the truth; and Scripture, the written Word of God, is indeed the Word of truth. Yet the search for truth and for its clear expression is an obligation no responsible educator and writer, least of all a Christian one, can evade. All truth is of God. It is easy to say those words; to endeavor to apply them consistently and comprehensively is difficult.

The essays collected in this volume have to do with that endeavor. They range in subject matter from biblical topics, education, and social issues to mountain climbing and the arts. But they all share a relationship to God's truth. In Christ, in Scripture, and to a degree in the natural order, God makes his truth known. Moreover, the stream of history testifies to the continuing action of him who, though he is the Judge of this "bent world," so loved it as to become the Saviour of all who believe in him. No more can be claimed for these pages than that they attempt to see certain aspects of life and thought in relation to the Lord of truth and the Word of truth.

Editing these pages has made me aware of occasional repetition in thought if not in words. Some but not all such repetition has been removed, for I am a teacher and good teaching uses repetition to drive lessons home. Most of the selections first appeared in *Christianity Today* either as editorials or as articles. A number of them were originally sermons or addresses, and thus were extensively revised before publication. As to the mountaineering essays, the reader should know that, though my lifelong love of mountains has led to many ascents, my attainments as a mountaineer are only modest. It is in these essays that the inclination of a teacher and preacher to glean illustrations from personal experience crops up. And there is good precedent for the analogy of mountain travel to Christian life. Reginald Heber speaks of a "noble army, men and boys, the matron and the maid" [who] "climbed the steep ascent of heaven through peril, toil and pain"; John Bunyan draws lessons from the sojourn of Christian and Hopeful in the Delectable Mountains.

It was at the suggestion of Mr. Calvin P. Bulthuis, Vice-President and Editor-in-Chief of the William B. Eerdmans Publishing Company, that I undertook the collection and editing of these essays. For his advice regarding their choice and arrangement I am grateful. I also thank the publications referred to under Acknowledgments for their generosity in giving permission to reprint the material, most of it copyright, that makes up the book.

Arlington, Virginia   FRANK E. GAEBELEIN
May, 1967

Acknowledgments

Grateful acknowledgment is made to the following for kindly allowing the use of copyright material in this book:

Christianity Today for "Let's Return to God's Word," "The Educating Power of the Bible," "Education and the Evangelical Minority," "A Strategy for Christian Education," "What Are We Doing to Our Youth?," "Youth and the Church," "The Centrality of the Word of God in Education," "The Greatest Educational Force," "Christian Faith and National Power," "Evangelicals and Public Affairs," "Christian Compassion," "Civil Rights and Christian Concern," "Cigarettes and the Stewardship of the Body," "Abstinence Makes Sense," "The Christian's Intellectual Life," "The Aesthetic Problem," "The Debasement of Taste," "The Christian Use of Leisure," "Music in Christian Education," "Is the Church Finished?," "The Minister and His Work," "The Continuing Power of the Resurrection," "What Is the Church For?," "Christ Comes Twice";

The Sunday School Times for the four essays entitled "Mountain Views";

The American Alpine Journal for "An Unrealized Hazard";

His, student magazine of Inter-Varsity Christian Fellowship, for "What Is Truth?";

Moody Monthly for "Why the Bible?"

Appreciation is also expressed to the National Union of Christian Schools for permission to use "Christian Schools and Citizenship," and to *The Gordon Review* for "The Idea of Excellence and Our Obligation to It."

The essays on "Civil Rights and Christian Concern" and "The Aesthetic Problem" also appear in *A Christianity Today Reader*, published by Meredith Press, 1967.

Contents

PREFACE   5

PART 1: EDUCATION AND YOUTH

1. Christian Schools and Citizenship   13
2. A Strategy for Christian Education   23
3. Education and the Evangelical Minority   30
4. The Educating Power of the Bible   35
5. The Centrality of the Word of God in Education   40
6. What Are We Doing to Our Youth?   49
7. Youth and the Church   53
8. The Greatest Educational Force   57

PART 2: PUBLIC AFFAIRS AND SOCIAL CONCERN

9. Christian Faith and National Power   63
10. Evangelicals and Public Affairs   67
11. Christian Compassion   71
12. Civil Rights and Christian Concern   75
13. Cigarettes and the Stewardship of the Body   79
14. Abstinence Makes Sense   84

PART 3: CULTURE AND TASTE

15. The Christian's Intellectual Life   91
16. The Idea of Excellence and Our Obligation to It   97
17. The Aesthetic Problem   105

18. The Debasement of Taste   113
19. The Christian Use of Leisure   119
20. Music in Christian Education   123

PART 4: MOUNTAIN CLIMBING

21. Mountain Views   133
22. An Unrealized Hazard   150

PART 5: THE CHURCH'S TASK AND MESSAGE

23. Is the Church Finished?   157
24. What Is the Church For?   160
25. The Minister and His Work   164
26. What Is Truth?   171
27. Why the Bible?   180
28. Let's Return to God's Word   186
29. The Continuing Power of the Resurrection   190
30. Christ Comes Twice   195

EDUCATION AND YOUTH

One

CHRISTIAN SCHOOLS AND CITIZENSHIP

Since the Greeks, who were pioneers in the field, using the schools to train youth in citizenship has been one of the accepted goals of education. Some may wonder, therefore, what there is new to say about it. But newness is not the measure of value, and there is much that is pertinent and urgent in the relation of our Christian schools to citizenship.

It is not just the threat of Communism which compels attention to our subject. It is the kind of age in which we live and also the lateness of the hour. In an address before the American Headmasters Association in 1962, Dr. John Carleton of Westminster School, London, said that we have reached a stage in world history when eschatology might well be made a required subject for examination. His remark points to the urgency of the times and the need for rethinking the purposes of our Christian schools, including their responsibility for citizenship education.

What is citizenship? Recently I looked up the words "citizen" and "citizenship" in Webster's Unabridged Dictionary. First I read the obvious — that a citizen is "a member of a state; . . . a native or naturalized person who owes allegiance to a government and is entitled to reciprocal protection from it and to enjoyment of the rights of citizenship" . . . and that citizenship is "the status of being a citizen." But along with the obvious, Webster points out the distinction between the word "citizen," as already defined, and the word "subject," the latter sometimes going beyond membership in and loyalty to a state and implying complete "subjection to a person as to a monarch." And that brought me up with a start, because it reminded me that for Christian education citizenship has a dual aspect. Every one of us Christian teachers and pupils holds citizenship not only nationally but also in the greater and deeper sense of being a subject of our Lord and Master, Jesus Christ.

The meaning of this is strikingly illustrated by the Apostle Paul. We know from the Acts that he valued highly his free-born Roman citizenship. But he had another allegiance. Christ was his absolute Lord, and in this relationship Paul gladly counted himself a bond slave. When, after his arrest in Jerusalem, he stood before the Sanhedrin, you will recall that he began his defense like this: "Men and brethren, I have lived before God in all good conscience until this day." But the verb he used was *politeuo,* which means to "live as a citizen." What he was saying was that he had lived conscientiously as God's citizen, as a member of God's commonwealth. And in his letter to the Philippians, who prided themselves on their citizenship of a Roman colony, Paul reminded them of their obligation to make their citizenship on earth consistent with their heavenly allegiance. "Only let," he urged them, "your manner of life [again the word is *politeuo*] be as it becomes the gospel of Christ."

It is this duality of citizenship that marks the radical difference between secular and Christian education. Secular education sees the child as a citizen of one world only; Christian education sees the child as a citizen of heaven as well as of earth, a citizen in eternity as well as in time.

Christian education is far more than moral and ethical education; it is education in subjection, in captivity to the living God, who first loved us that we might love him, who sent his Son to die for the ungodly, even for us who were dead in trespasses and sins. It grows out of the Gospel of grace and newness of life through the crucified and risen Christ, not out of a system whereby man is saved by what he does. Yet Christian education, if true to its master textbook, the Bible, sees the critical importance of morality and ethics as the essential outward evidence of the faith of the heart. True to its Lord's drastic demand, it looks for the regeneration, not just the reformation, of youth; and it expects the manner of life, the citizenship of its students, to be in conformity with him from whom all authority and government derive and who is the truth as well as the way and the life. Therefore, Christian education has got to be concerned through and through with integrity, which means the practical everyday doing of the truth, without which there can be no noble and effective citizenship.

In his diary, Jonathan Edwards, while a student at Yale back in the eighteenth century, wrote in a birthday entry in his teens: "Resolved first, that every man should do right. Resolved second, that I would do right whether anyone else in the world does or does not." To endeavor to instill integrity like this as the rock-bottom basis of citizenship is the task of the Christian school. But, you ask, "How? How are we to do it?" Now there are two main answers to this question. Both of them apply to Christian education.

There is, first, citizenship education through specific courses — and our Christian schools have them — such as civics, problems of American democracy, world history, American history, and the like, courses that come under the broad heading of social science. No one would deny the place of such subjects in the curriculum. I confess, however, to a feeling of concern about what seems to have become almost an over-emphasis on the social studies in our American education. If I were to sort into piles the teacher applications that come to my desk, I should have on the one hand a large number from social science majors, a considerably lesser number from English majors and from mathematics and science candidates, few indeed from modern language teachers, and hardly ever an application from a Latin teacher.

Social studies are essential. Our students must know the history of the country and its mode of government, and, under the stress of our times, they must be taught about Communism. But let us not deceive ourselves into thinking that by these courses alone our schools are discharging their whole obligation in respect to citizenship. It is one of our American failings to think that through passing a law or prescribing a course in our schools we have solved some human and social problem, when all we have done is to declare it off bounds or to impart some information about it. In a discussion of citizenship education, Sir Richard Livingstone quotes Pascal's saying, "How far it is from the knowledge to the love of God!" And then he wryly comments, "How far it is from civics to citizenship!"

So we come to the second answer to the question, "How to educate for citizenship." To put it very briefly, it is this: Citizenship education comes through the whole program of the school, not just through what is taught in one part of the curriculum. As the article on "Citizenship Education" in the *Encyclopedia of Educational Research* declares at its close: "Our present state of knowledge regarding citizenship education indicates that it is not a program for social studies classes alone, but that the total school and the total community are involved."

Observe the emphasis upon the word "total," for therein lies the challenge and opportunity for the Christian independent school. If citizenship education comes from the whole program, then it can best be done by schools that are under no limitations as to the range and depth of that program. We who are committed to Christian education enjoy in our democracy the priceless freedom really to educate the child in body, mind, and spirit. We can do what the public schools in their growing and almost all-pervasive secularization cannot do; we can teach the unity of all truth under God; we can bring our youth to the source of the values upon which responsible citizenship that serves God and country and fellow man depends — the values set forth in the Bible, the Word of God, and practiced in informed and responsible Christian living.

The Christian school must have the Bible at the center of its curriculum. Taught with a constant awareness of its relation to every other field of knowledge, its truths brought to bear upon the life of the pupil and the world around him, the Bible course should play a powerful part in building attitudes of good citizenship. Conversely, for a Christian school to be content with mediocre Bible teaching — and I am afraid that at times some of us have fallen into this snare — may breed serious lack of concern for social and moral responsibility.

Some time ago, Dr. James Bryant Conant, former President of Harvard University, whose books on public education are so

16

well worth reading, gave a lecture in the American Heritage Series at the University of Colorado. In it, he contrasted two modes of thought: the empirical-inductive method and the theoretical-deductive method. The first, he explained, is the method of trial and error, of experimentation, and he showed how it is linked to our American pioneer, inventive heritage. The second, the theoretical-deductive kind of thinking, he set forth as characteristic of the European mind, which is more concerned with principles than with practice. By way of illustration, Dr. Conant told how, after an address he gave in Stuttgart, he was asked how American schools educate for citizenship. He replied by telling something of our social studies courses and methods. "But," persisted his questioner, "what about your metaphysical principles?"

This brought laughter from the audience. But you and I know that, when it comes to the great questions of faith and morality, the values which undergird true and godly citizenship, the trial-and-error, empirical method will not do. Secular education would derive values only from a sociological, humanistic context; Christian education knows that there are God-given, revealed absolutes in the spiritual and moral realm — Christian metaphysical principles, if you will — and that it is our duty to teach them according to the Word of God, and, with increasing insight and dedication, to apply them to every area of life and citizenship.

But again the question arises — How? How are we in Christian education to do this? What can we teachers and administrators, we parents and trustees, all of us who have a deep and lifelong commitment to Christian schools, do about this so vitally important matter of citizenship training? The answer to that question may be put in a single sentence: Let the Christian independent school be what it potentially is; let it be both independent and Christian in the fullest sense. Now there are some corollaries of that sentence. For the Christian independent school to be both independent and Christian in the fullest sense, in all-out dedication to what it really is under God, means several things.

17

For one thing, it means that we must stop confusing our independence with isolationism, our freedom to teach the faith once delivered to the saints with parochialism and separatism. Yes, we are different. That is our right and our privilege. Yes, with our God-centered philosophy we are non-conformists to the secularism that surrounds us. We are determined not to let worldly education "squeeze" us "into its mold." We are, and always shall be, a minority. But let us never forget the power of a minority, provided that it maintains contact with the majority, and persistently and courageously and lovingly lets its voice be heard.

May I ask some pointed questions of you, my colleagues in Christian education? How wide are your community and educational associations? Are you and your schools members of regional and national organizations? Do you have a part in the work of such organizations? Do you ever speak out for your convictions in a meeting or from the floor at a secular gathering? Such nation-wide groups as the National Association of Independent Schools, such a group as the Council for Religion in Independent Schools, with a constituency of some 550 leading schools from the Atlantic to the Pacific that are concerned about religious teaching, or the Educational Records Bureau, a leading testing service, sponsored largely by independent schools, need the support of Christian schools.

Let us remember that we cannot influence others unless we know them and talk to them. As Lester DeKoster says in his excellent book, *Communism and Christian Faith,* "A Christian social order must be oriented to society as it is. This calls for intimate and sustained insight into the ... ways of the world ... an insight acquired by *involvement* [the word is rightly italicized] as well as by study."

The often quoted remark of Henry Varley to Dwight L. Moody, "The world has yet to see what God can do through a man wholly yielded to him," may be applied to us, for the educational world has yet to see what God can do with schools, not just with one but with many schools, wholly yielded to him — schools that, though a minority, dare to be involved courageously and articulately with the education of their day.

Does this have anything to do with citizenship? Of course it does. The very essence of citizenship is concern for those about us and involvement with them. If a school is a good citizen of the broad educational community, there is bound to be a carry-over to the pupils.

Let the Christian independent school really be what it is called to be. And that spells in capital letters the obligation to excellence. I am convinced that the school that insists on excellence to the glory of God, that demands hard work of its pupils — and of its teachers also — is well on the way to effective citizenship education.

But the obligation to excellence relates to more than academic studies; it entails the extra-curricular program, the administration, the discipline, and the total atmosphere of the school. A student organization, capably supervised, which does not mean over-supervised but conducted so as to allow students to learn by their mistakes as well as by their successes, gives far better training in citizenship than student replicas of the U. N. or miniature political conventions. The latter are bound to be theoretical and unreal, beyond the actual experience of children; the former is within the scope of their day-by-day living. If your school has a student organization, is it capable of holding an orderly, effective meeting of all your students without the presence of the principal or of any teacher, even though ordinarily a faculty adviser is present?

Athletics and interschool athletics — in which I thoroughly believe — are an undoubted training ground for citizenship if integrated with the Christian purpose of the school. So are all the other activities — clubs, music, and the like. Here the New Testament gives us the master text in Colossians 3:17: "Whatsoever you do in word or in deed, do all in the name of the Lord Jesus Christ, giving thanks to God and the Father by him." Nor should we, as practicing educators, ever underestimate the place of discipline in citizenship education. One of the things I have learned in forty years of living and working with boys is that, despite their adolescent tendency to rebel, down underneath they respect those who hold them to standards.

19

And surely you agree with me that the school that provides an understanding and just framework of discipline is already doing much in the way of effective citizenship education.

All these things contribute to the influence of the school as a whole, the influence of the school as a community. Atmosphere may seem an intangible thing. Yet it is one of the chief realities of any school. Said the Chairman of the Evaluating Committee when Stony Brook last came up for re-accreditation under the Middle States Association, "I don't have to be on a campus very long before I know even without visiting classes what kind of school it is." Just to belong to a school that is a true community, close-knit, seriously concerned for standards and values, is for a boy or girl a precious experience in citizenship.

Think how great in this respect our opportunity is! Ours is the privilege, through the mutual dedication of teachers, administrators, parents, trustees, and young people, to develop schools that have a pervasive Christian atmosphere.

But this is a subtle matter. Christian atmosphere is not the result of self-conscious contriving; under the mysterious leading of the Holy Spirit, it comes out of the total life of a community that places Christ first and that, despite human weaknesses and the sin that so easily besets us, seeks earnestly to do the will of God. A school does not just *have* an atmosphere; it *is* an atmosphere. Sometimes the school whose atmosphere speaks most eloquently for God is least conscious of its influence. Moreover, it must also be said, not only of teachers and pupils but also of parents and trustees, that in their own practice of the presence of God, in their personal adherence to the high values of Christian citizenship, in their concern for influencing the society in which they live, they have a share in the development of an atmosphere that nurtures Christian citizenship. Nor ought we to overlook the fact that nothing less than sacrificial giving and support of Christian education is demanded of parents and trustees. Let me say bluntly that when a constituency which provides the support of Christian education is content to keep its schools in a poor-relation status, it is giving pupils and teachers negative training in citizenship.

Finally, there is a caution that must go with our concern for citizenship education in this time when our national security is being threatened. The caution is this. Along with our commitment to freedom, we must, despite our abhorrence of Communism, learn to put first things first. Why, after all, are we concerned about building character and imparting to our young people the values that make for good citizenship? Is it for the sake of the sovereign God who according to Scripture ordains the power of man and of the state, the God from whom all the values that underlie true citizenship derive? Or is it that, fearful that our cherished liberty and security — yes, our economic security and our high material standard of living — might be lost, we think of citizenship education as useful primarily for our own human ends, for the preservation of our status quo?

What, then, comes first? What has the highest priority? Why must we be concerned with Christian citizenship?

Speaking at the 200th anniversary of Nassau Hall at Princeton, Dr. John Baillie of Edinburgh quoted the Westminster Shorter Catechism: "What is the chief end of man? The chief end of man is to glorify God and to enjoy him forever." Then he said, "It is within the context of that question and answer that that which we call our Western civilization has developed, and I believe our civilization to be doomed to swift disintegration and decay if it should cease to be aware of itself as standing within that context."

Near the border of Alberta and British Columbia in Canada there is a magnificent mountain crowned with glittering glacial ice and snow. Its name is Mt. Edith Cavell from the heroic British nurse who in the First World War faced a German firing squad in Belgium for the sake of her country. Her last words have found their place in history. They are these: "Standing as I do, in view of God and of eternity, I realize that patriotism is not enough." As Christians we should be patriots; but as Christians we are more than patriots. This is a day when a revival of honest patriotism, when a strong stand for freedom, when the will to plan and work and suffer, if need be, for our nation are of high importance. But for this day, when we stand, as we do, at the beginning of the space age with nuclear catastrophe round the corner, patriotism is not by itself enough. And by the same token citizenship is not by itself enough.

What is enough? Commitment to the living God through his Son our Lord Jesus Christ; education according to the truth set forth in the Bible; schools conducted, youth taught, in the fear of the Lord, which is the beginning of noble citizenship as well as of wisdom; life lived not only for human ends but first of all to the glory of God.

Address at the Annual Convention of the National Union of Christian Schools, 1962.

— *Directory of Christian Schools,* 1962-1963

Two

A STRATEGY
FOR CHRISTIAN EDUCATION

Americans have long been education-conscious, and in recent years this consciousness has grown until education now occupies a central place in national life. A President who began his career as a school teacher has made education one of the primary concerns of his administration. The National Defense Education Act of 1958, the 1963 Higher Education Facilities Act, the Anti-Poverty Act of 1964, and the School Aid Act of 1965 all involve the federal government in education far more widely than ever before. Dissent from concern for schools and youth is methodological rather than principial. No one — the Christian least of all — is against better education.

If education is a national concern, it is even more a Christian one. To a unique extent, Christianity is a teaching religion. Its founder was called "Teacher"; the twelve to whom he entrusted his mission were pupils, and he commissioned them to go into the world and make pupils of all nations, teaching them to do all he had taught. In America, just as abroad, the Church is the alma mater of education. But the mother has been overshadowed by the child. If we liken the kinds of education in our democracy to mountain ranges, the Rockies are the public schools and state-supported colleges, dwarfing the Appalachians of the private schools and colleges. Yet the latter are no mean feature of the educational landscape — not in a day when one out of every seven children is enrolled in a parochial or independent school.

What of evangelical attitudes toward education in a time when Congress has passed one multi-million-dollar education act after another? Are evangelical Christian schools and colleges, numerically but a fractional part of the minority of parochial and independent education, to remain bound to the status quo in a kind of paralyzed awe at the bigness of government involvement and at the vast sums being accumulated by top-ranking private institutions? For them to do so may spell decline if not ultimate extinction. On the other hand, if Christian education really faces its position vis-à-vis the colossus of government-supported public education and the necessity of greatly increasing its support from private sources, and if it goes forward with fidelity to its biblical distinctives, it may face its future with hope.

Consider, then, some matters about which Christian educators must do some hard thinking. Like its predecessor, the 1963 Higher Education Facilities Act, the 1965 School Aid Act reaches out a helping hand to religious schools of all kinds. By an ingenious compromise, this legislation opens the door for private education — parochial schools, parent-controlled Christian day schools, and other religious and private schools — indirectly to receive some government help. To be sure, the aid is not to be given to schools themselves but to pupils and teachers through such things as provision of textbooks and apparatus, radio and TV programs, supplementary educational centers, visiting-teacher programs, and shared time. Nevertheless, the door to use of federal funds for religious and nonpublic education has been propped open.

The *Washington Post* spoke of "this mingling of public and private education as a softening of the lines that ideally ought to separate church and state." But the "softening" is actually a breach, insignificant though it seem, in the wall of separation of church and state. It may be that the breach was inevitable and that, after years of tension about the use of tax funds for religious schools, something had to give. The extent to which church-state separation has been penetrated will be determined by Supreme Court decisions that are bound to come.

Amid these tensions, the position of the Christian school and college sometimes borders on the schizophrenic. Too many Christian colleges have accepted government subsidy in one way or another — as for dormitories, for research projects, for surplus materials — to make their avowal of fidelity to church-state separation entirely convincing. There are, to be sure, some few

24

Christian institutions that for the sake of principle have consistently refused all manner of government subsidy. But let us have no illusions about the record of most evangelical schools and colleges in this respect.

This being the case, what is the Christian school and college to do in this day of rising educational costs? In a time when $10,000 salaries for public school teachers and $15,000 salaries for college professors are no longer a rarity, when the cost of a college education is beginning to approach $3,000 annually and may in a decade reach $4,000, when all kinds of teaching aids from language laboratories to complicated scientific apparatus are required, when academic pressures have pushed back into the last years of the first-rate secondary school the freshman year of college through the Advanced Placement program, and graduate school techniques have been moved back into the upper classes of college, some Christian institutions are not just in second or third place in the academic race; they are in danger of being lapped by their publicly supported competitors. To be sure, many an evangelical school or college claims to be on a par with its public counterpart and bases this claim on accreditation, which some Christian institutions naïvely consider the promised land but which is only a preliminary step toward academic excellence.

Let it be plainly said that the evangelical community by and large has much to learn about support of its educational institutions. The Achilles' heel of many a Christian day school, to cite one aspect of the problem, is the inordinately rapid turnover of faculty, an inevitability in view of minimal salaries. Because of inadequate support from a constituency that values evangelical Christian education so lightly as to keep it on a starvation diet, a disturbing number of Christian institutions merely subsist. A reformation in evangelical education is overdue — a reformation not of doctrine but of support.

The Christian educator stands between the Scylla of martyrdom for refusal of public aid and the Charybdis of acceptance of such aid. Little wonder if, faced with the plain fact of the lawful distribution of public funds for education, he seeks for his school and pupils their share. To do otherwise might mean

25

sacrificing the quality of Christian schooling for what, under the realities of education in America, may become a doctrinaire position, unless the Supreme Court declares unconstitutional recently legislated support of private religious schools and colleges.

One of the scandals of evangelicalism is the second-rate quality of many a school bearing this name. Even a cursory glance through a recently published directory of Christian higher institutions shows many an evangelical school that offers little but the rudiments of an acceptable education. Quality is not a matter of lavish facilities. It depends on good teaching, continuity of faculty and administrative service, adequate living conditions, and essential equipment, especially the library. Evangelicalism has not always supplied its schools with these necessities. Recognizing that they live, as all men do, in an imperfect society, many evangelical educators will reason that to withhold from their institutions and pupils public benefits legally available is to deprive them of indispensable assistance. Yet the acceptance of such funds must not short-circuit private support, lest the Christian school ultimately find itself dominated by the state.

On the other hand, if Christian educators believe that for principle's sake they cannot under any circumstances accept government aid, then they are duty-bound to find ways greatly to increase support from their constituencies and also to tap new sources of aid.

Turn now to a subject to which evangelicals give comparatively little attention — the public school. That there is tension between many evangelicals and public education is undeniable. In some communities evangelicals have responded by beginning their own Christian day schools or by developing within their denominational framework Protestant parochial schools. Other Christian parents want for their children the experience of public education, where they are in daily contact with children of all faiths or none. Such parents believe that, through training at home and in church, supplemented later perhaps by a Christian college, their children can be adequately grounded in the faith. But what evangelicals cannot do is to dismiss public

26

education as beyond the pale of Christian concern. If for no other reason than that some of their tax dollars go into public education, evangelicals have their share of responsibility for the public schools. But above material considerations is the spiritual need of American youth in public education. If evangelicals believe what they profess, how in the name of Christian compassion can they be unconcerned about youth in the public schools?

"But," someone says, "with restrictions resulting from recent Supreme Court decisions, how can there be any real evangelical involvement in public education?" The answer lies in two directions: the teacher and the curriculum. No teacher speaks out of a religious and ideological vacuum. Every teacher has some commitment, whether religious or secular. It is all very well to theorize about objectivity and neutrality in teaching. To a degree, these are essential in public education. But in the deeper sense there is really no such thing as complete objectivity or absolute neutrality. What a person *is* cannot be prevented from showing through his teaching.

Christian teachers ought to consider public school teaching a vocation to which God may call them. On accepting such a call, they ought to be meticulous about observing state-prescribed restrictions against religious indoctrination. Here they have a Christian duty to obey the powers that be and to set an example for teachers with naturalistic presuppositions. And devoted Christian teachers will deal with their pupils in Christian love. Moreover, outside the classroom they have liberty to propagate their faith. They may work with church youth groups and bear witness to their beliefs. What they stand for in the community is no secret to their pupils.

But what of the place of Scripture in public education? The following statement from Mr. Justice Clark's majority opinion in *Abington* v. *Schempp* actually opens the door for the teaching of the Bible in the public school classroom: "One's education is not complete without a study of comparative religion or the history of religion. . . . It certainly may be said that the Bible is worthy of study for its literary and historic qualities. Nothing we have said here indicates that such *study of the Bible* [italics ours] or of religion, when presented objectively as part of a secular program of education, may not be effected consistent with the First Amendment." Recently this option has been discussed in the national press. Granted that evangelical Christians do not consider the mere reading and study of the Bible as being everything they desire, nevertheless through such study thousands of pupils who have never seriously read the Book of books and who might never do so will be brought into personal confrontation with it.

In this pluralistic society, neither evangelicals nor any other Christian group can demand that the Bible be read and studied from their particular point of view. But they can agree on a study of the Book as literature, provided that this study is not conditioned by particular theories of the origin or composition of Scripture.

Some, however, may say that such use of the Bible in public education is not worth the time it takes. As Rolfe Lanier Hunt of the Department of Church and Public School Relations of the NCC has asked, "Will learning the facts about a play by Shakespeare assure a love of literature of drama? Will memorizing the Ten Commandments assure behavior obedient to them?" In either case, the answer is a qualified negative, with the qualification bulking largest for the Ten Commandments or any other portion of Scripture. Scripture is not Shakespeare. To read and learn Shakespeare may or may not create love for this great writer. But Shakespeare cannot change the human heart. Scripture is of a different order; it is the inspired Word of God. Perhaps the time has come for evangelicals to realize that their explanations and helps in understanding Scripture are not indispensable. Perhaps they should learn to rely on the promise of Isaiah 55, "My word . . . shall not return unto me void." Perhaps they should be in the forefront of those advocating the exposure of youth to the Bible through literary study. Courses of this kind will also help dispel the all too prevalent biblical illiteracy. And, in a number of communities, notably in Indiana and in Texas, they are now being given in public schools.

There is much unfinished business on the docket of Christian education. The time is overdue for group thinking about Christian involvement in the broader aspects of American education. Now is the time for evangelical educators, representing elementary and secondary schools, liberal arts and Bible colleges, Bible institutes and seminaries, to meet for open-minded discussion of a strategy for Christian education. Such a strategy would relate to such things as the response of Christian education to federal aid in the light of church-state relations, the position of evangelicals respecting public schools, and the imperative need of arousing Christians to the necessity of greater and more sacrificial support of their schools and colleges. It would enlist the best thinking of the evangelical community. Those who represent the theological convictions out of which education in America grew must give up their parochialism and face together the responsibility for the larger witness to which God is calling them. Let there be no mistake about it: the day when any part of Christian education can "go it alone" without seeking counsel from the whole of Christian education is past.

— *Christianity Today,* May 7, 1965

Three

EDUCATION
AND THE EVANGELICAL MINORITY

In an editorial introduction to a recent issue of *Columbia College Today* featuring the place of religion at the college, George Charles Keller tells how an undergraduate asked him one day what this alumni publication was going to discuss. When told that the subject would be "Religion on the Campus," the student, obviously taken aback, exclaimed: "But, sir, there is none." The young man went on to say that, while some students attended church services, took religion courses, or belonged to religious clubs, their motivations came from anything but "a deep sense that they owed reverence to a God who created the world and is still involved in everything men do or try to be."

With this Mr. Keller expressed substantial agreement, saying, "Religion in the traditional sense of formally offering awe and gratitude to a mysterious, omnipresent being has departed for the most part from college campuses. . . . However, religion in a new sense is growing rapidly at American colleges." And he defined religion as "mainly a personal quest by young men for some reasonable guidelines for their own actions and clues to the meaning of history."

Unquestionably the place of religion in school and college is one of the livelier subjects of the time. The churches are probing it; witness Professor William Hordern's articles published simultaneously in *Presbyterian Life, The Lutheran,* and *The Episcopalian.* In the "Survey of the Political and Religious Attitudes of American College Students" that appeared in the *National Review,* Protestant students in comparison with Catholic students made a poor showing in stability of faith, and one Protestant church college had the highest rate of apostasy of any college polled.

As for the public schools, the religious discussion continues in the wake of the Supreme Court decision on Bible reading and prayer. When a parent visiting his child's classroom in a Rochester (N.Y.) elementary school sees on the blackboard, "The heavens declare the glory of nature," and is told by the teacher that the quotation of the Nineteenth Psalm was revised at the principal's request, the role of religion in public education is still very much confused.

The instinct that leads Americans to be concerned about religion in education is a sound one. Few if any institutions in a nation influence its citizenry more than its schools; and in America, with education for all, this influence is especially pervasive. More than one in every four in our 188 million population is enrolled in public and private schools and colleges. Only recently the Educational Policies Commission of the National Education Association announced as the new goal for the nation's schools "universal opportunity" for *all* youth to have two years' education beyond high school at "non-selective" public colleges on a tuitionless basis together with provision when needed of the expense of living away from home. Moreover, the rise in independent school attendance from 1899-1900, when 91 per cent of children were in public and 9 per cent in private schools, to 1962-63, when only 85 per cent were in public schools and 15 per cent in private schools (the vast majority of which are religious), underlines widespread parental concern for the spiritual training of youth.

Against this background, where does Protestant Christian education, particularly that of evangelical persuasion, stand? The first answer to the question is statistical. If the great majority of the 15 per cent minority (6.7 million in total) of elementary and secondary school pupils are in Roman Catholic parochial schools, as they are, and if only a comparatively small number of the remaining private schools are evangelical, then such schools are only a minority of a minority — and a tiny one at that. For the colleges, the situation is broadly comparable; Christian institutions are again in the minority and those that are evangelical are again a sub-minority.

But is Protestant Christian education in general — and the

drop-in-the-bucket evangelical minority in particular — therefore negligible? Are evangelicals so far behind educationally that their influence may be written off? To both questions the answer is an emphatic No.

Look once more at the background: the increasing number of religion courses in many colleges, yet the undergraduate saying of religion on his campus, "But, sir, there is none"; the repudiation of supernatural religion, and its redefinition as a quest for guidelines and clues to the meaning of history — all this is far from authentic religion even according to the broad Judeo-Christian tradition, let alone its expression in the grand particularities of the historic evangelical faith. It is rather the search for a philosophy and the desire for purpose and for personal identification. And the result may be that, with all the meticulously objective study of religion, the student may merely work out his own philosophy of life, which will be, as Canon Bryan Green has said, only "My-anity" and not vital Christianity.

But what about faith on the campus? To overlook its presence and to belittle its relevance betokens a kind of spiritual myopia. Not all practicing Catholics and Jews worship only by force of habit. Not all Protestants are superficial formalists. There is on the American campus a committed minority (faculty as well as students) that crosses denominational lines and includes in a practical biblical ecumenism those who out of a personal, saving encounter with Jesus Christ recognize their oneness with all believers and who find the Bible essential spiritual food as well as the infallible rule of faith and practice. Measured against the millions in higher education, this minority is numerically insignificant. Measured against the little group of disciples who turned the world upside down, it is large. And it is worldwide. At Oxford, Cambridge, and other British universities, among college and university students in Europe, Asia, Africa, Australia, South America, and the Orient, there is a remnant of Christian students and teachers. And where it is found, there even on the secular campus *is* religion in its worldwide, biblical aspect.

Protestant colleges are of two kinds: those that are church-related and those that, while independent of denominational control, yet maintain a thorough-going Christian position. In the first group are the colleges — and their number is considerable — that differ little from the private secular colleges. To be sure, they have departments of Bible and religion, chapel services, and religious emphasis weeks (a singularly patronizing term); but these are peripheral to an education in other respects indistinguishable from its secular counterpart. Here the adjective "church-related" betrays a kind of second-cousin-once-removed relationship quite different from whole-hearted commitment of administration and faculty to a denominational and theological position.

Yet there are also some church-related colleges that are unreservedly committed to the biblical world view and that, along with the group of evangelical but denominationally unaligned colleges, comprise institutionally a conservative Christian minority in higher education. For this minority, Christ and the Scriptures are central to the program and the unity of all truth in God is a major premise. For them the faculty is a fellowship of believers, not an eclectic company made up of Christians, adherents of non-Christian religions, and more or less benevolent unbelievers. In a day of doctrinal indifference they hold to the biblical doctrines of supernatural Christianity and know their position to be compatible with good scholarship. While the number of such colleges is small yet growing, their influence for the Kingdom far transcends their size. From them has come significant national and world evangelical leadership. They too are a part, and a not inconsiderable one, of the believing remnant in education today.

But any estimate of religion in education cannot be confined to the colleges and universities. It must also take account of the formative years of childhood and the crucial years of adolescence. Here the lines are sharply drawn. By constitutional interpretation public schools are secular. But independent schools are free to use their independence for Christian education as fully as they desire. The number of Christian day schools, both denominational and parent-controlled, is growing. Some boarding schools are thoroughly committed to the unity of education in Christ and the Bible. Would that more of the non-Roman Catholic independent schools might be like-minded!

As for public education, it would be a mistake to assume that because of its religious neutrality it is devoid of a faithful remnant. Wherever a Christian who knows whom he has believed and trusts the Bible as the Word of God teaches in a public school classroom, there is something of Christ.

Yes, there is religion on the campus — university and college, secondary and elementary school, public and private. Through the believing remnant, Christianity is in education every day. It is there for the age-old purpose of witness and response. Let objective college courses in religion continue. They have their place in the academic program. But their upsurge on the secular campus is of lesser significance than the consistent witness of the believing remnant to the living God of the Scriptures and to his Son. Amid the sophistication, moral ambiguity, and longing for personal fulfillment, the unchanging Christ, when lifted up in his saving reality, still draws youth to himself.

One of the encouraging signs of our day is that American education, apart from the public school, is more ready to hear the Gospel of Jesus Christ than it was twenty years ago. And of those who are hearing it on the campus, some, like C. S. Lewis, are "surprised by joy." The reception accorded Billy Graham at secular colleges and universities is genuinely significant; with commendable liberalism many a college chapel is more open to evangelical preaching than in the past. Organizations such as the Inter-Varsity Christian Fellowship and Campus Crusade for Christ that have opportunities parallel to those of the denominational student ministries should take full advantage of them.

Let the Christian remnant in education proclaim their Lord with conviction and by faithful word and consistent life. The God who brought out of academic communities in the past a Luther and a Calvin, a Wesley and an Edwards, a Drummond and a Mott, may be trusted to bring forth his leaders for today.

— *Christianity Today,* February 28, 1964

Four

THE EDUCATING POWER OF THE BIBLE

The Bible and education are indissolubly united. To understand something of their relation requires at least passing reference to what each is. The word "education" comes not, as commonly supposed, from the Latin *educere* (to "lead" or "draw forth") but from *educare* (to "rear" or "bring up"). The distinction is not minor for the Christian. If education means nothing more than drawing out what is already within the person, then regeneration is unnecessary and the atoning work of Christ may be bypassed. But if to "educate" means to "rear" or "bring up," then the creation of new life within the person through the Spirit's use of the Word of God is recognized, and education becomes in its Christian aspect the nurture of the new man in Christ Jesus.

For this nurture the Bible is by its very nature indispensable. When the Apostle Paul said to Timothy, "...from childhood you have been acquainted with the sacred writings which are able to instruct you for salvation through faith in Christ Jesus" (II Tim. 3:15), he was pointing not only to the educating power of the Bible but also to its function in regeneration, even as the Apostle Peter declared: "You have been born anew, not of perishable seed but of imperishable, through the living and abiding word of God" (I Pet. 1:23). Moreover, when Paul went on to say, "All scripture is inspired of God and profitable for teaching, for reproof, for correction, and for training in righteousness, that the man of God may be complete, equipped for every good work" (II Tim. 3:16, 17), he was explaining both the nature of Scripture — the book "inspired by God" (literally, "God-breathed") and its function — the formation of Christian maturity effective in good works.

Such is the essential educating power of the Bible. And with-

35

out clear recognition of this power there can be no Christian education. Whenever education, even though church-sponsored, departs from a primary biblical frame of reference, it becomes secularized. It is obvious that by far the greater part of present-day education is divorced from the Bible. Equally obvious but less clearly understood is the not uncommon attempt by religious groups to maintain Christian education with the Bible relegated to a secondary or merely peripheral role. In fact, the low estate of Christian belief on many church-related campuses today may well be the result of undervaluing the educating power of Scripture.

Likewise the strange biblical illiteracy of multitudes of church members points to failure of pulpit and Sunday school to teach the people adequately the unique, God-breathed sourcebook of their salvation. Surely one of the causes of much spiritual ineffectiveness in Protestantism today is that those who should be "the people of the Book" do not even know the Book. Not only so, but many of them are content to be ignorant of it.

Outwardly the state of the Bible was never more flourishing than now. This twentieth century may even be known by future church historians as a century of Bible translations. Circulation of Scripture is at a peak. The American Bible Society, which accounts for about 60 per cent of total worldwide Scripture distribution by the United Bible Societies, was responsible in 1962 for the circulation of 31,509,821 copies of Scripture in whole or in part. And in addition to this figure there are the millions of copies circulated apart from the Bible societies. Sales of the King James Version have not decreased, while the sales of the newer versions (the Revised Standard Version, Phillips, and the New English Bible) are soaring. Yet this is also a day when modern literature and entertainment deal with the great questions of human life and destiny as if the Bible had never been written and as if the Ten Commandments and the ethics of the New Testament were unknown, a day when distinguished writers glorify the very vices the Bible denounces. No wonder that the morality set forth in Scripture is flouted on every hand.

Thus we face the paradox of such a Bible-possessing generation as ours being so little affected by biblical teaching. Yet the resolution of the paradox may be comparatively simple. To own a Bible and even to read it is not enough. The Book must be believed, obeyed, and lived by daily. Its truth is not just to be admired but to be done. For as the Apostle John said, "He that doeth truth cometh to the light" (John 3:21a).

An enduring revival will come only through devoted, informed, and trusting use of the Bible. Neither evangelistic campaigns, liturgy, social action, mysticism, nor charismatic experiences can revive and reform the Church unless the Bible is dominant in the minds and hearts of both clergy and laity. At this point, candor compels the admission that evangelicals cannot be exempted from the charge of possessing and even knowing the Bible without being willing to submit to its power. Orthodoxy for orthodoxy's sake can never be a substitute for doing God's truth.

Nevertheless, the educating power of the Bible remains unabated for all who will submit to it. Consider the incomparable record of its translations. Other ethnic religions have their sacred books, but none of them has a translation history like that of the Bible. From the Greek Septuagint down through the Latin Vulgate, the Anglo-Saxon versions, the Middle English of Wycliffe, and the translations of Tyndale and Coverdale — to name only a part of the provenance of our English Bible, the Book has been translated and retranslated. Not only so, but those who have had it in their mother tongue have been moved to give it to others in *their* mother tongue. The result is that, according to the American Bible Society, by the end of last year the entire Bible had been translated into 228 languages, and parts of it into 1202 languages and dialects.

These are more than statistics. They are evidence that the Bible is beyond question the greatest single educating force the world has ever known. The missionary enterprise is inescapably educational. "Go ye therefore," said the risen Lord, "and teach all nations..." (Matthew 28:19). And at its heart is the Bible. The great outreach of missions since Zinzendorf has been through the Scriptures, so that the history of missions is in good part the history of Bible translation. Only the Scriptures so lay hold upon men and women as to compel them to go to the dark places of the earth, to stone-age savages and nomad tribes, with the Gospel. Constrained by the love of Christ, the pioneer missionary must first reduce the primitive language to writing and then, after years of effort, translate the Scriptures into that language. In this way, the door to literacy and thus to enlightenment has been opened to countless millions who would otherwise have remained in intellectual as well as spiritual darkness. No other book can compare in educating power with the Bible.

By the same token, the Bible is the ecumenical book par excellence. Despite the widespread superficiality of its use, God is working mightily through it today. Not all Christians agree about the ecumenical movement. But no Christian, no matter how deep his conservative and evangelical commitment, can deny the essential ecumenicity of the Word of God.

With this kind of ecumenicity all who acknowledge the educating power of the Bible should agree. Thus when word comes from an authoritative Roman Catholic source (Father Eugene H. Maly, president of the Catholic Bible Association and an official theologian of Vatican Council II) that "a version of the Bible acceptable alike to Catholics, Orthodox, and Protestants of the English-speaking world . . . has become a definite possibility," evangelicals, knowing the power of the Bible, cannot but be interested.

The objections of evangelicals to reunion of Protestantism and Rome are indeed rooted in their deepest convictions. Their grave concern that the price of such reunion would be the abandonment of the very heart of the Reformation faith is well founded. But these objections do not apply to a common English Bible open to all who call themselves Christians. Such a new "Vulgate" would represent a kind of ecumenicity that any Christian would have difficulty in opposing. To be sure, the realization of a Bible of this kind is by no means round the corner. Moreover, when and if it comes, it would undoubtedly not supplant in worship and liturgy the great existing versions. Yet it might find wider use than expected, and its educating power under God could not be restricted. For if, as John Robinson of Leyden truly said, "the Lord has more truth and light yet to break forth out of his holy word," we may trust God to use every faithful translation of that Word for the continuing enlightenment of all who read it.

— *Christianity Today,* November 22, 1963

Five

THE CENTRALITY OF
THE WORD OF GOD IN EDUCATION

A careful look at our subject, "The Centrality of the Word of God in Education," provides a clue to its treatment. Quite evidently, two things stand side by side — the Word of God and education. The first of the two, "the Word of God," needs close definition; the second, "education," must be brought to focus upon the particular kind of education with which we are here concerned, namely, that which is called "Christian."

Consider the phrase "the Word of God." Though a synonym for the Bible, this by no means exhausts its meaning. In a Supreme Court opinion, Justice Holmes once said, "A word is not a crystal, transparent and unchanged; it is the skin of a living thought, and may vary greatly in color and content, according to the time when, and the circumstances under which, it is used." Keeping this in mind, we may identify three aspects of "the Word of God" in its relationship to education. They are: first, the written Word of God, the Bible; second, the Word of God manifest in creation; and third, the Word of God incarnate in our Lord Jesus Christ.

We begin with the Word of God as Scripture. Among Christians in general and evangelical Christians in particular, the Word of God has long been equated with the Bible. The equation, though it does not exhaust the meaning of the phrase, is fully justified because it is made again and again in the Bible. And for Christian education Scripture is the integrating center. But why so? Why not theology? Or why not the officially sanctioned philosophy of a great doctor of the church, as in Roman Catholic institutions with their Thomism?

Before dismissing this question as being so obvious as not to require an answer, let us look beneath the surface to see some reasons why this book, and no other, must be central in Christian education.

One reason is the sheer, unapproachable greatness of the written Word of God. Considered just as a book, it holds the first place by reason of the criterion voiced in the treatise *On the Sublime,* traditionally ascribed to Longinus: "That is really great which bears a repeated examination, and which it is difficult or rather impossible to withstand, and the memory of which is strong and hard to efface.... For when men of different pursuits, lives, ambitions, ages, languages, hold identical views on one and the same subject, then that verdict which results, so to speak, from a concert of discordant elements makes our faith in the subject of admiration strong and unassailable." This is the doctrine of literary criticism known as the Law of Universal Consent and it applies to the Bible as literature. Over and above any other piece of world literature from Homer down through Virgil, Dante, Cervantes, Shakespeare, Milton, and Goethe, no book has been more fully acknowledged as great simply as a book than the Bible.

Let no Christian educator ever apologize to the sophisticated of the educational world for giving to the Bible the highest place. To take as the center of the curriculum the one book among all the other great books to which alone the superlative "greatest" can without challenge be uniquely applied — this is neither narrow nor naïve. Rather it is simply good judgment to center on the best rather than on the second best.

But there is a deeper reason why the written Word of God must be at the heart of our schools and colleges, and that is its authority as the inspired, inerrant Word of God. At this point plain speaking is in order. The current movement to express the Christian faith in contemporary, understandable terms, so that the people whom we must reach for Christ will know what we are talking about, deserves support. We should rejoice at the renaissance of good and enlightened scholarship among evangelicals that is sometimes called neo-evangelicalism. But at the same time we must not overlook the evidence that there is current among some evangelicals a subtle erosion of the doctrine of the infallibility of Scripture that is highly illogical as well as dangerous.

It is illogical for this reason. We live in a day when archaeology has confirmed Scripture to such a degree that the number of alleged discrepancies used by destructive critics of the past in their efforts to discredit Scripture has been greatly reduced. Those who over the years have held a suspended judgment regarding Bible difficulties, while still adhering to the infallibility of the book, have found question after question cleared up by new knowledge. Therefore, with all our openness of mind and emphasis on scholarship, we need to be careful to maintain the historic, orthodox view of Scripture as being infallible (a view not to be equated with the dictation, mechanical theory of inspiration, but one held by our Lord and the apostles). And we need to maintain this position against neo-orthodox views of the Bible that may infiltrate even the Christian school and college. Let us by all means redefine and restate the evangelical position, but never at the cost of yielding any essential part of the authority of the Bible.

Another reason why Scripture must be at the heart of education concerns its indispensable critical function. In a day of debased values and satisfaction with the second and even third rate, education requires a standard and point of reference by which the cheapened standards of our day may be judged.

Writing at the beginning of the industrial revolution in England, Wordsworth declared: ". . . a multitude of causes, unknown to former times, are now acting with a combined force to blunt the discriminating powers of the mind, and, unfitting it for all voluntary exertion, to reduce it to a state of almost savage torpor." And he went on to speak of the literature of violence and sensationalism of his day. But now, under the impact of far greater changes and forces than any industrial revolution, and beset with the debasement of plain, everyday decency, this violent age in which we live has far more need of discriminating judgment than the age of Wordsworth.

No other book can fulfill this critical, discriminating function like the Word of God. As the writer of Hebrews said, "the word of God is quick, and powerful, and sharper than any two-edged sword, piercing even to the dividing asunder of soul and spirit, and of the joints and marrow, and is a discerner [Greek, *kritikos*] of the thoughts and intents of the heart." In a time which Sir Richard Livingstone has rightly called "The Age without Standards," the Bible alone qualifies as the supreme critic of life and thought.

To use the phrase of Gerard Manley Hopkins, ours is "the bent world." The "bent" refers to the distortion of sin that stems from the fall and runs through all of life. And from this "bent," even Christian education is no exception. We do not always realize that this distortion affects areas of knowledge and education to different degrees. As Emil Brunner has pointed out, the twist resulting from sin is most marked in the humane subjects like theology, philosophy, history, and literature. It is less marked in areas like physics and chemistry, and in mathematics it approaches zero. Thus there is Christian theology, Christian philosophy, or Christian literature, but not Christian mathematics. It is in the humanities that the curricula in our schools and colleges have their strongest emphasis; and it is here that the critical, penetrating, revealing function of the Bible is most needed.

Now true as this principle is, in practice it needs care and courage. Let us in Christian education be fearless enough in our reliance on the critical function of Scripture to subject even our cherished formulations about the Bible to its own divine, discriminating judgment. Let us see in the Bible's searching scrutiny that some of the neat and pat systems we have been teaching may need revision. For there is yet more truth to be learned from the Bible. Let us therefore seek to the glory of God to develop in our students a proper critical-mindedness that subjects all the thinking and formulations of men to the ultimate principles and judgments of the divine *kritikos*, the Word of God. The seventeenth chapter of Acts gives us a significant example of this function of Scripture. The Christians at Berea, we are told, "were more noble than those at Thessalonica, in that they received the word [in this case doubtless the *kerygma* or proclamation of the Gospel] with all readiness of mind, and searched the scriptures daily, whether those

43

things were so." In other words, these Christians subjected even the apostolic preaching to the test of the Scriptures. And, it should be pointed out, there is an extension of this Berean principle beyond even doctrine. This is not to say that technical knowledge in science or any other field must be checked point by point with the Bible, but that in respect to ultimates, to the comprehensive frame of reference in Christ by whom (Col. 1:17) "all things consist [hold together]," the Bible is the final critic.

There is still another reason why the Bible must be at the heart of Christian education. It relates to the all-important matter of knowing and finding the truth. The natural tendency of man is to go his own way. He is prone unwittingly to slip into the error of assuming that human effort, working independently, leads to the truth. Thus man tends to become in relation to knowledge what Emile Cailliet calls "a pseudo-maker," with truth coming at the end of a process of human rationalization.

On the contrary, the whole thrust of the Bible is different. It does not give us truth through rationalization but through revelation. Truth is not something worked out by men; it is received by faith and then acted upon. Here the biblical method of knowledge is what Anselm of Canterbury expressed in these words —"Credo ut intelligam" ("I believe that I may understand") — a principle voiced also by Augustine some six hundred years before Anselm, when he wrote, "Nisi credaritis, non intellegistis" ("Unless you believe, you will not come to know"). This insight, so thoroughly biblical, was not, as Professor J. Harris Harbison of Princeton University pointed out, any "advocacy of blind faith. It was the testimony of one of the greatest minds in Christian history to the fact that truth can never be grasped by a man's mind alone." And going back to Solomon, we must add this: "The fear of the Lord is the beginning of wisdom"; for there can be no "fear of the Lord" without humble belief and reverential trust.

Moreover, basic knowledge in any field, including scientific insight, has this ultimate revelational factor. As Cailliet in his book, *The Recovery of Purpose,* again reminds us, reality was "there in the first place and then literally happened" to man.

Witness, among many instances, Archimedes with his un-expected discovery of the principle of hydrostatics and Newton's experience that led to a comprehension of the law of gravitation. In the deepest sense, knowledge is something that "happens to man" by way of faith acting upon faith; it is not "spun out of the human self." And the Bible is *the* book of faith leading to truth.

But the great phrase, "the Word of God," has two other meanings aside from Scripture itself. These also must be seen in relation to Christian education. Consider creation as the Word of God, or nature as God's other book. The Psalmist says: "By the word of the Lord were the heavens made; and all the host of them by the breath of his mouth. . . . For he spake, and it was done" (33:6, 9). And the prologue of John's Gospel declares: "In the beginning was the Word. . . . All things were made by him; and without him was not any thing made that was made." So also, "The heavens declare the glory of God" (Psa. 19:1); and, looking about us in the natural world, we may see "the invisible things of him . . . even his eternal power and Godhead" (Rom. 1:20) .

Now this aspect of "the Word of God" has its clear implications for the curriculum of the Christian school and college. In this age of science and mathematics, we must, if we are to communicate with those about us, speak their language. The schedules of some evangelical educational institutions are loaded with courses in Bible, theology, language, philosophy, music, and the like. However, must not more room be made for science and mathematics, so that Christian graduates will be literate in contemporary, world-changing concepts of science and mathematics?

There are those who charge Christian education with narrowness and provincialism. In his book *Christian Faith and Higher Education,* Nels Ferré says, "Some writers . . . advocate the teaching of the Bible as central to the Christian curric-ulum. When this suggestion is understood . . . namely, that the Bible is the source book and standard of all other truth, the Bible is wronged and higher education is imperialistically attacked. This is parochialism of the first order." But if Dr.

Ferré had read his reference, *Christian Education in a Democracy,* carefully, he would have seen that nowhere is the Bible set up as the sourcebook of all other truth. Instead he would have seen that the Bible invites Christian education "to range over the realm of science in all its forms, over the treasures of literature, the mansions of philosophy and theology, and the beauty of music and art; according to its [the Bible's] warrant, all the best that has been thought and said and done by men through the ages ... comes within the province" of Christian education.

We look again at the phrase "the Word of God," as we think about its third meaning. While the Bible is assuredly "the Word of God" and while creation is God's other book, the Word of God is something even greater than these. As every Christian knows, the Word of God is also Christ. To the first two meanings of "the Word of God" Christ sustains an indissoluble and pre-eminent relation. In Hebrews 4:12-16 we see the writer's thought moving from what many commentators take to be the written Word, to the Son of God, the incarnate Word. The plain fact is that Christian education must always see the Bible not as an end in itself but as pointing to Christ who is its theme and subject from Genesis to Revelation.

The moment we lose sight of the truth that the incarnate Word, the eternal Son of God, is greater than and above the written Word which, with all its inspiration and infallibility, is still a product of the Holy Spirit, we are in danger of bibliolatry. As Adolph Saphir said, "By Bibliolatry I understand the tendency of separating in the first place the Book from the Person of Jesus Christ, and in the second from the Holy Spirit, and of thus substituting the Book for Him who is alone the light and guide of the Church." For a school or college to assert that it is Bible-centered is in itself no guarantee of power. It is even possible for the orthodox to become so devoted to details of biblical scholarship as to lose sight of him whom the Bible is all about.

When the Bible is really at the center in education, the one chief subject is not just the Bible in its linguistic and historic or even doctrinal sense. It is, over and above this, Jesus Christ.

As Professor T. W. Manson remarked in a comment on Ephesians 4:20 (where Paul says by way of exhortation, "You have not so learned Christ"), "The writer speaks of learning Christ as you might learn algebra or French. It is an extraordinary statement and one, I think, that goes to the heart of the matter." Spencer Leeson, Bishop of Peterborough in England, in his Bampton Lectures at Oxford, titled *Christian Education,* heads his chapter on "The Content of Christian Education" with the eighth verse of Hebrews 13: "Jesus Christ the same yesterday, and today, and forever." And how does a college or any educational institution teach Christ? In the classroom, yes, but also by the kind of administration and teachers it has. By its ethical, disciplinary, and social tone, and by all that it is and stands for, it teaches Christ.

In conclusion, consider the implications of our discussion. For the whole enterprise of Christian education these implications point in one direction — toward the continuing obligation of excellence. At the Fiftieth Anniversary of the Cum Laude Society in 1956, the late Dr. Claude Fuess, Principal Emeritus of Phillips Academy at Andover, Massachusetts, spoke on the subject, "The Curse of Mediocrity." In his comment on the prevailing satisfaction with the average and second rate in our schools and colleges he quoted this evaluation: "Dismal and hopeless mediocrity is the most serious menace to present-day primary and secondary education in America." And, we might add, if mediocrity will not do for public and secular education, it is doubly a curse for evangelicals contentedly to tolerate it in education that is committed unreservedly to the Word of God.

Someone will say, "But we in Christian education just do not have resources in equipment and endowment that secular institutions have." That is true. In this world's goods Christian education is comparatively poor. But good taste and high personal standards and lofty intellectual achievement are not confined to the rich. Granted that the quest for excellence is a continuing one and that humility forbids anyone a feeling that he has arrived, the Christian college, along with every other part of Christian education, cannot evade the unremitting pursuit of excellence to the glory of God.

According to Hudson Taylor, every work for God has three stages — Impossible, Difficult, Done. Most Christian schools and colleges have been through the "impossible" stage, when it hardly seemed that they could ever begin. All of them are in the "difficult" stage right now, and here they stay; to make the Word of God central in education, and to do it without mediocrity and with a growing attainment of excellence, is an uphill struggle. Only at the final time of accounting, when we stand before the throne of him whose Name is called "the Word of God," will "Done" be written over our endeavors to make the Word of God the center of education.

Address at the annual convention of the Accrediting Association of Bible Colleges, 1960.

— *Christianity Today,* May 9, 1960

Six

WHAT ARE WE DOING TO OUR YOUTH?

"Unto us a child is born." So the prophet heralded in words close to the heart of every parent God's greatest gift to lost humanity. No wonder Paul, contemplating the glorious fulfillment of Isaiah's announcement, exclaimed, "Thanks be unto God for his unspeakable gift." When God came into human life he entrusted his only begotten Son to an earthly home, and the Saviour was reared by a godly mother and her devout husband. Immeasurably above us by reason of his deity, the Child of Bethlehem has an essential bond with us through his humanity. The joyous exclamation, "Unto us a child is born," re-echoes whenever the Giver of all life entrusts a new life to a father and mother.

The bond between our imperfect humanity and the perfect Son of God lends poignancy to the youth problem. The sad paradox is that children who should be our greatest joy bring sorrow to many a home. Among the domestic problems of our nation, none is greater than that of delinquent youth. It is ironic that the announcement of the Population Reference Bureau that this year a total of 3.1 million persons in the United States will celebrate their seventeenth birthday — nearly one million more than the number of seventeen-year-olds in 1963 — is accompanied by a note of foreboding, as it points to inevitable social problems of which delinquency is foremost. The increase of crimes committed by American young people has been almost three times as great as the phenomenal growth in adolescent population. Though reasons why youth go astray are complex, it is possible to isolate some of the basic factors leading to juvenile delinquency and, having isolated them, to point to remedies.

Chief among these factors is the deprivation of youth. And

49

contributing to their deprivation is their exploitation. Few generations of children have been more pampered materially than this one. On the other hand, few have been so deprived of what they most need for growth into strong and responsible maturity.

But how are they being exploited and deprived? Answers to the question shout at us from every side. Recent decades have witnessed the mushroom growth of the cult of the teen-ager, so that we are fast becoming a teen-age society. Mass-media publicity of latest adolescent fads; bigger allowances and promotion of charge accounts for youngsters (teen-age income now totals $12 billion annually) ; automobiles as teen-age status symbols; special telephones for offspring of the affluent; emotional and sexual over-stimulation through the moral looseness of the day and through the social precocity demanded of children by ambitious parents — these are only a few symptoms of the exploitation of youth.

The result is that young people have been led to believe, as *Time* has said, that the teen-age years are the apex of life instead of an essential step toward adulthood. Thus millions of our youth are being cheated out of precious experiences of childhood which, once past, can never be regained. Adult pressures, often selfish and at best thoughtless, emphasize the outward accouterments of maturity. But growth must come from within. The process of maturation cannot be hurried, and to give immature youth the prerogatives of maturity before they are ready to handle them leads to trouble.

Along with emphasis upon material things and the forcing of maturity, there goes the deprivation of youth. This transcends even the loss of authentic childhood experiences. The deepest deprivation is emotional and spiritual. It may be that future historians of education will judge as a critical defect of the American home and school in the second half of our century the failure to understand that for youth authority is both creative and essential. Parents and schools that lack the moral fortitude to say "no" to children are depriving them of the very foundation of emotional stability. Behind the burst of juvenile criminality is disrespect for law, and behind disrespect for law is disrespect for authority.

In a powerful phrase in Second Thessalonians, the Apostle Paul speaks of "the mystery of lawlessness." Though eschatological, the phrase has a present significance. (It is significant that in certain New Testament contexts the word "mystery" refers to what has become an open secret.) Behind the lawlessness among youth today, whether in Harlem riots or in Labor Day disorders of more privileged youth at Hampton Beach, New Hampshire, or Seaside, Oregon, the open secret is want of respect for authority.

The Fifth Commandment declares, "Honor thy father and thy mother: that thy days may be long upon the land which the Lord thy God giveth thee." But for children to obey this commandment, parents must pay a price. They must be worthy of honor. They must not cheat in matters of integrity. They must have the strength to demand of children the respect and obedience that are a true expression of love. Let parents never think that they can cut corners in ethics, nourish their prejudices, live chiefly for the things of this world, maintain a religious and even an evangelical front, and at the same time receive from clear-eyed youth honor and obedience.

One of the sociological phenomena in America is that in great cities like New York and San Francisco that have a considerable Chinese community, juvenile delinquency among these people is practically unknown. The acknowledged reason is the firm pattern of respect in the Chinese family. Surely it is a reproach to a nominally Christian nation that children from homes of a non-Christian culture have a moral stability lacking in our youth.

Isaiah said of the virgin-born Child, "His name shall be called Immanuel." And now, when it is hard to be a Christian and hard also to be a Christian parent, let believing fathers and mothers find strength and comfort in knowing that the Holy Child who came into this lost, burdened, sinful world on the first Christmas is their "Immanuel." He is never more truly "God with us" than when we strive humbly and in accord with the Scriptures to lead our children to that loving respect and

51

obedience that are the basis of character strong enough to withstand the winds of the shoddy ethics and moral relativism blowing so persistently in our society.

Children must be evangelized; they must know the way of salvation. The Child of Bethlehem was called not only "Immanuel" but also "Jesus, for he shall save his people from their sins." Yet Christian nurture remains an inescapable obligation. Parents and schools that fail to instill respect for authority have yet to take the first step in preparing youth to face "the mystery of lawlessness" so prevalent today.

— *Christianity Today,* December 4, 1964

Seven

YOUTH AND THE CHURCH

Among the recent discussions of the problems of American youth today, *Teen-Age Tyranny* (William Morrow and Company, 1963), by Fred Hechinger, education editor of *The New York Times,* and his wife, Grace Hechinger, takes high rank for the intelligence and candor with which it faces the problem. It is not comfortable reading; out of abundant documentation it shows things as they are among the rank and file, not of socially and economically underprivileged boys and girls, but of our young people who are being schooled in the most expensive educational system any nation has ever had and whose material advantages exceed those of any of their predecessors in our history. Because of the hard common sense with which it deals with adolescent mores today, *Teen-Age Tyranny* is of special interest to parents, ministers, teachers, and youth counselors.

For the discerning Christian reader one sentence in the book stands out as even more disturbing than the facts about youthful violence and promiscuity. The Hechingers disavow any religious orientation of their discussion. But when in a scant page and a half they do refer to religion and youth, they offer this thought-provoking observation: "Since 84% of today's teen-agers are church members and more than half attend church regularly, they could undoubtedly be influenced strongly by religious values." That youth in general are not so influenced confronts the reader on almost every page. Moreover, because a book like this is largely a transcript from life, the failure of the Church to counteract an adolescent culture that has given up the common morality of the Judeo-Christian tradition can be substantiated in almost every community in the country.

Why this failure? Why do the churches, by and large, have so little influence upon our youth? Answers to such questions as these must be found. For what shall it profit the churches to claim as members 84 per cent of the youth, when so many of these young people are living by sub-Christian and even pagan standards?

The question may be answered in part by another quotation from the Hechingers: "Teen-age values are inevitably determined by the adult values around them." Or, as Professor Henry Steele Commager put it, "The American has boundless faith in the new generation, is willing to make almost any sacrifices for it except those required by self-restraint" *(The American Mind).* It is plain that youthful conduct reflects adult standards or lack of them. But to admit the truism only leads to another question: "Why has the Church not influenced those many adults whose own moral failures are reflected in our youth?"

At this point evangelicals are likely to say that the answer is clear. Thinking of the prevalence in many pulpits of liberalism with its denial of the radical need for regeneration, they are inclined to blame the ineffectiveness of the churches in producing a stronger morality upon one thing — failure to preach the Gospel. That there is truth in the charge is undeniable. But that it is not the whole truth is equally undeniable. Honesty compels the admission that evangelical churches where the Gospel is faithfully proclaimed also have a good many grave moral problems among their youth and among their adults as well. The Gospel is indeed "the power of God unto salvation," but to be believed it must first be understood. And to be understood it must be communicated effectively and in the conviction and power of the Holy Spirit.

Consequently, the answer to the problem of a high rate of church membership and a low standard of morality among young people is not so simple as some have thought. In fact, it goes deeper even than the assumption, too common among evangelical Christians, that witness is only a matter of words.

Let there be no misunderstanding. The presentation of the Gospel in words is primary and essential. The story of salvation through the death and resurrection of Christ must be told in complete fidelity to the biblical sources and in words that the hearer can understand. Yet a preacher, Sunday school teacher, or youth leader may be as orthodox as Scripture itself and fail to reach young people. Orthodoxy just for orthodoxy's sake neither wins souls nor nurtures Christ's flock. The message must indeed be understood if it is to be obeyed. And that it can reach even the most thoughtless teen-ager has been shown by such a movement as Young Life, which is primarily concerned with effective communication of the Gospel of Christ to high school boys and girls by leaders who love youth, who speak to them out of the conviction of personal experience, and who are first willing to take the time to know them and listen to them. By the same token, it can be effectively presented by pastors, teachers, youth leaders, and, above all, by parents who will make a like effort to understand and be understood.

But the communication of the saving truth of Christ also has, as has already been suggested, a non-verbal aspect. Words are essential for communication. But they do not stand alone. They must be backed by conviction and reinforced by the reality of consistent living. Even the clearest communication intellectually may be vitiated by a lack of love and Christian concern.

Youth longs for reality. It understands instinctively the language of the heart that underlies and transcends the form of words. As Pascal said, "The heart has its reasons, which reason does not know." Youth knows those reasons. But when it sees adult selfishness and unconcern and when it has set for it examples of moral flabbiness and lack of spiritual discipline, it will not listen to the message of the Gospel that has apparently done so little for those who profess it.

Another thing needs to be said, not as an exculpation of the Church's failure to influence more of its youth but as a reminder of a profound biblical truth. The Gospel, as the apostle declared, is "a savor of life unto life and death unto death." Its faithful proclamation does not inevitably bring salvation. Not all will be reached by it. Not all can be compelled to accept it. God respects individual responsibility far more than we do. Not even the most dedicated and skillful preacher or teacher, nor the most devoted parent, is successful in reaching every child. Yet grant-

55

ing this, the disinterest of youth in the Church is so great as to cause deepest concern.

Still other factors must be considered. Evangelism, primary though it is, must be supplemented by activity. Souls, just as bodies, grow strong by exercise. An easy religion has little appeal to youth. The church that caters to youth through parties and recreation and never faces them with the stringent demands of the Gospel and its application to the hard moral and social issues of the times will not build godly character.

The key to the youth problem, as to every other aspect of life and service, is Christ. But the possession and effective use of that key are costly. In the words of Samuel Rutherford, "There are some who would have Christ cheap; they would have him without the cross. But the price will not come down" (*The Letters of Samuel Rutherford*). So with the meeting of youth's needs in a time of sagging morality and increasing secularism. The price of presenting the living Christ to youth in words backed by life and integrity makes high demands upon Church and individual. Behind the rebellion and dubious moral values of many young people is a true yet unrecognized search for identity. If the Church is failing to influence youth deeply and is not turning them to paths of righteousness, it may well be because of adult failure to show forth Christ in life as well as in word.

— *Christianity Today,* January 3, 1964

Eight
THE GREATEST EDUCATIONAL FORCE

By any thoughtful estimate, education is a major function of our society. Speaking to representatives of land-grant and agricultural colleges President Johnson said, "The first work of these times and the first work of our society is education." America is indeed education-conscious. It may well be true that no nation has ever spent more money on its schools and on its youth than ours.

Yet something is wrong. Deep-seated discontent and explosive unrest trouble the American soul. Along with material prosperity and a constantly advancing level of education, there are symptoms in our society that cannot be masked.

Among the ugliest of them is the criminality that afflicts American life. Contrary to the common opinion that cities and slums are chiefly responsible for the upswing in crime, FBI statistics show that crime is moving to the suburbs. Looking at the nation as a whole, it is shocking to realize that crime is outstripping our population growth fivefold. The rise of 8 per cent in population since 1958 has been left far behind by the 40 per cent increase in crime.

But what of juvenile criminality, to use the blunt word rather than the euphemistic "delinquency"? Arrests of youths under eighteen years of age for criminal acts have been rising annually for many years. It is sobering that our young people are responsible for a disproportionate share of the national crime rate.

As one contemplates these facts, particularly those respecting juvenile delinquency, he is driven to ask, Why? Answers are manifold. But among them there is one that cannot be evaded. The problem of crime is intimately related to education. That not all is well with our schools is evident. Yet to place upon them the chief responsibility for moral slippage and mounting crime is neither fair nor accurate.

What is the greatest single educational agency? And by the same token, where does the greatest responsibility for youth rest? Some may point to the elementary and secondary school (public or private, secular or Christian) or the college and university (state-supported, private, or church-related). Others may attribute to the informal but all-pervasive molders of human personality — television, radio, stage and screen, news-papers, periodicals, and popular books of the day — the greatest educational influence. Still others will look, perhaps wistfully, to the Church.

But while all these are potent educational forces, none of them is the greatest single educational force. This distinction belongs to the home. The most influential teachers, whether they recognize it or not, are parents. To say this is not to belittle the vital importance of good schools and able teachers. It is not in any way to minimize the strategic place of Christian schools and colleges, which indeed are a dynamic spiritual minority in the great system of American education. But it is to place the emphasis educationally where the Bible places it — upon parents and upon the family. And the urgent, in-escapable responsibility of teaching God's truth to our children found throughout the Old Testament is summarized in Deuter-onomy: "These words . . . shall be in thine heart: and thou shalt teach them diligently unto thy children, and shalt talk of them when thou sittest in thine house, and when thou walkest by the way, and when thou liest down, and when thou risest up" (6:6, 7). The New Testament continues this emphasis, partic-ularly in the Pauline epistles. Indeed, no book of the Bible is without some sort of reference to the family.

This is an age of revolution in race relations, in morality, and in technology. And perhaps the most important, though largely unrecognized, revolution has to do with the family and the home. The integrity of the American home, using the word "integrity" in its root sense of wholeness, has been breached. The God-fearing family that united parents and children in a common life in the home no longer characterizes our nation.

There are many reasons for this. They include the move from rural to urban society with the trend to megalopolis, a car for nearly everyone (teen-age children included), the vast number of alcoholics (many of them women in the home), increasing divorce, preoccupation with show business and with having fun almost anywhere but at home. The paradox is that with greater leisure for true home life than ever before, we have less home life than ever before. What this may mean was put in one sentence by Carle Zimmerman, when he said, "If there were no A-bomb or H-bomb, we would have to recognize the fact that no civilization has ever survived the disintegration of its home life."

For better or worse, the home wields more crucial influence upon youth than does school or college. The same is true of parents. No kindergarten teacher, grade school teacher, high school teacher, or college professor, however effective, can surpass the influence of a devoted Christian father or mother. Contrariwise, one shudders at the influence for evil that may be exercised by unworthy parents. The reason is that what psychologists call "feeling tones" are deeper and more pervasive in the emotional setting of the home than in the school. J. Edgar Hoover was right when he said in an article written expressly for teachers, "There is but one way to eliminate juvenile delinquency. That is by providing each child in America with competent parents."

What does it mean to be a competent parent? Or, to put the question in another way, What does it mean to have a good and godly home? It means first of all to have a home where each parent is a Christian — not just a nominal Christian but a person who has by God's grace experienced through faith in Jesus Christ the miracle of regeneration. It means also a home where parents are serving God, whatever their calling in life may be. In relation to the Church, parents cannot stand on the sidelines as non-participants. Persons are saved individually, but Christianity is a social religion.

Again, no home can be effective for the nurture of its children in grace and character unless the Bible and prayer are at its

59

heart. It is God's plan for every Christian home to be a church that has an altar with the Bible upon it.

Christian parents no less than their secular neighbors need to be recalled to their inescapable educational responsibility. They are not exempt from the erosion of values in the materialistic and pleasure-obsessed society of today. Softness in discipline, lack of respect, self-indulgence, are just as damaging in Christian homes as in the homes of unbelievers. One of the greatest anchors that boys and girls may have is respect for parents based upon love. Saving faith in Jesus Christ is indeed essential. But Christian youth can fall into delinquency along with their secular companions. Accompanying the maturing child's natural desire for independence, particularly in adolescence, there is a fundamental need for a firm structure of authority in the home. Without such authority, exercised in loving concern and responded to in respectful obedience, emotional maturity may be blighted.

To be an effective parent these days is not easy. It requires much love and faith and self-restraint to train a child in the way he should go. And if Christian parents ask with Paul, "Who is sufficient for these things?," let them also say with him, "Our sufficiency is of God."

— *Christianity Today,* August 28, 1964

PUBLIC AFFAIRS
AND SOCIAL CONCERN

Nine

CHRISTIAN FAITH
AND NATIONAL POWER

What, if anything, has Christianity to do with American national power? Consider the relation of the Christian faith to the establishment of the country. The founders of the New England colonies came to these shores because of religious conviction. Here they sought and found freedom to worship God according to conscience. Our national independence has two chief sources: on the one hand, the deism of men like Jefferson and Paine, who were strongly influenced by the French enlightenment and the philosophy of John Locke; on the other hand, the Calvinism of our Puritan, Scotch-Irish, French-Huguenot, and Dutch forebears. The Calvinistic idea of the sovereignty of God, and its correlate of man, responsible to God with a dignity upon which others may not trespass, was one of the great formative influences in our national origin. As the historian Leopold von Ranke said, "John Calvin was the virtual founder of America."

While the dominant spiritual force in America has been, and still is, Protestant Christianity, constitutionally Protestantism has no more official status than Roman Catholicism, Judaism, Mormonism, or Christian Science. Yet this does not imply that America is committed to secularism. The First Amendment to the Constitution was in no sense meant to banish religion but simply to keep the government from establishing any church. Our founders openly acknowledged God and his sovereignty.

In "Young John Adams," a study that appeared in *The Atlantic Monthly,* Catherine Drinker Bowen tells of an incident at the Continental Congress, meeting in Carpenters Hall, Philadelphia, in 1774. A clergyman was asked to lead the Congress in prayer. A report came that Gage's soldiers had seized the powder stores "at some town near Boston." The author tells how the Reverend Mr. Duché in his black gown walked into the hall the next morning, followed by a clerk bearing the Bible. He took his place before the desk and, after reading prayers, announced the Thirty-fifth Psalm. "He had a voice of great sweetness and warmth; he read slowly with no show of dramatics: 'Plead my cause, O Lord, with them that strive with me: fight against them that fight against me. Take hold of shield and buckler and stand up for mine help....' The effect was electric. Men bowed their heads and wept."

The acknowledgment of Almighty God is a part of our American tradition. Indeed, the public recognition of God is woven into the fabric of our national life. The inauguration of a president partakes of the nature of a solemn religious ceremony. There is deep meaning in the opening of Congress with prayer, even though to some it may seem an empty formality. The phrase "under God" in the flag salute and the motto "In God We Trust" on coins are things we take for granted. But in times of national emergency, as in the tragic experience of President Kennedy's assassination, the nation instinctively reaches out to God for help.

The founders of our country showed farsighted wisdom in providing such a clear safeguard against the establishment of religion in the First Amendment. But it must not be forgotten that the First Amendment also guarantees "the free exercise" of religion. Thus religious initiative is left to the people. Just as no man may be required to pay lip-service to the living God, so no man may be prevented from confessing and practicing his faith.

Christianity may exercise a vital and determinative influence in the nation, but only upon its own terms. It is never to be used merely to bolster patriotism, or just to support the political, economic, or military status quo. To think of finite man using the infinite God for his own ends is impious folly. Every nation, the United States included, stands under the judgment of God. It is, therefore, a great and dangerous perversion to consider the Christian faith merely as a kind of national convenience to be turned on when we need it and to be used for our own purposes. Christ is not subject to our direction; he directs us. God's ways are not our ways, nor his thoughts our thoughts. The power of Christianity in national life is effective only when men submit themselves humbly to God and to his Christ.

This is why churches, ministers, and laymen need to keep their priorities clear in these critical days. Christianity speaks to every aspect of life. It relates inevitably to spiritual and moral questions — and most issues having to do with human beings ultimately involve spiritual and moral issues, because man is a creature not only of time but also of eternity. But Christianity meets these issues primarily through regenerated persons who know that the Gospel of Jesus Christ is the power of God unto salvation and who are committed to his teaching every day and in every area of life.

What is the place of Christianity in American life today? The answer is that the great and awesome role of ministering the most powerful thing in the world belongs to the Church and to its members. Said the Apostle Paul, "I am not ashamed of the gospel of Christ: for it is the power of God unto salvation to every one that believeth." The word translated "power" is the Greek *dunamis,* from which we get the word "dynamite." Paul knew nothing of atomic power. But it may well be that, had he known it, he might have said that the Gospel is the atomic power of God unto salvation. Yet even that would be an understatement. The Gospel can do what even atomic power cannot do. It can take broken, disintegrating human lives and put them together into new persons reconciled to God and living in peace and love with other people. The Gospel creates. As Paul elsewhere says, "If any man be in Christ, he is a new creature: old things are passed away; behold, all things are become new."

Lord Acton's dictum that power tends to corrupt, and absolute power corrupts absolutely, admits of only one exception. There *is* an utterly incorruptible power. It is the power of the living Christ, the only uncorrupt person who ever lived, and his power is available for the healing of the nations.

The obligation of the churches and their members, stewards all of God's power, is so to proclaim and live the Gospel and all its implications as to send into the life of the nation men and women who are new beings in Christ — who know, not theoretically but practically, his power, and who are committed to personal witnessing and to applying his truth to shaping the society in which they live and work. Greater than all the military, industrial, and cultural resources of the nation are the spiritual forces resident in Christian men and women and in various forms of our national life.

— *Christianity Today,* July 2, 1965

Ten
EVANGELICALS AND PUBLIC AFFAIRS

In a time of ethical relativism, when social and moral problems beset us on every hand, evangelicals need to give careful thought to their position respecting public affairs. Committed to the Word of God and to a Lord who is the greatest of ethical teachers as well as the only Saviour from sin, they are spiritually among those to whom much has been given. Yet they have no occasion for pride, because humility is at the heart of the Gospel. If evangelicals rejoice in personal knowledge of Jesus Christ, their rejoicing must ever be mingled with honest realization that, apart from any merit of theirs, the divine Son of God who came to seek and to save the lost has sought and found them. Motivated not by fear of rejection by God but rather by love for him who has given them life everlasting — and love is always a stronger motive than fear — they are obligated to serve their Lord through serving their fellow men. Christ's saying, "Every one to whom much is given, of him will much be required..." (Luke 12:48b), applies with irresistible logic to them because of the riches of their spiritual heritage.

This being the case, there rests upon evangelical Christians a mandatory responsibility for unflagging interest in public affairs and for informed participation in them. That this is not nowadays a responsibility consistently discharged is a reproach to the evangelical cause and a denial of an important part of its heritage.

History bears voluminous witness to evangelical participation in public affairs. Reformation leaders, such as Luther, Calvin, and Knox, were concerned for the material as well as spiritual welfare of their fellow citizens and also for just government.

Moreover, as J. Wesley Bready has shown in *This Freedom, Whence?*, in early nineteenth-century England moral and social advances, such as the abolition of the slave trade, the restriction of child labor, and the mitigation of an inhumanly harsh penal code, came out of the Wesleyan revival. As for nineteenth-century America, Timothy Smith has demonstrated in *Revivalism and Social Reform* the same intimate relationship between evangelicalism and the amelioration of social abuses.

Although twentieth-century evangelicals in America have not always been so socially concerned as their predecessors, the accusation that they are almost devoid of such outreach is superficial. Aside from the foreign-missions movement, in which evangelicalism has been and still is the single most active force, the rescue missions dotting the nation's cities and offering physical as well as spiritual rehabilitation to human derelicts almost unreachable by other agencies are largely the product of evangelical initiative. Similarly, in the extremely difficult field of juvenile gangs, the most effective work, like that of Jim Vaus in Manhattan, is the direct result of evangelicalism. Despite their refusal to equate the social gospel with the Gospel of salvation through the work of Christ, evangelicals have always maintained some continuance of social concern.

Nevertheless, as Carl F. H. Henry said in *The Uneasy Conscience of Modern Fundamentalism,* they have lagged behind what is required of those to whom so much spiritual and doctrinal wealth has been committed. Today, nearly twenty years after Dr. Henry's book was written, their conscience is still uneasy, mostly because of sins of omission. That theirs is not the only uneasy conscience — for who in this day of multitudinous problems can claim a conscience completely unburdened — is beside the present discussion. Sufficient to say, evangelicals need to accept a greater share of responsibility for public affairs.

This they can do within the framework of their basic convictions and in a way wholly compatible with the clear teaching of the Bible. It is a principle held by many evangelicals that the Church should not enter into politics because the mission of the Church is the spiritual one of preaching the Gospel. Evangelicals believe with the Apostle Paul that there is only one Gospel — the Gospel of salvation through Jesus Christ who "died for our sins according to the scriptures . . . was buried, and . . . rose again the third day according to the scriptures" (I Cor. 15:3, 4). It is not unfounded fear that preoccupation with other matters, such as prohibition in the early decades of this century and now racial desegregation (important as it is), can almost usurp the primacy that belongs only to the Gospel. Nevertheless, the pendulum can swing too far in the other direction. And that this swing has occurred in the case of some evangelicals must be admitted.

According to much evangelical conviction, it is not fitting for the Church to inject itself into politics by taking sides in political campaigns, by telling members how to vote, or by lobbying in Congress and in state legislatures. But this does not mean that ministers and laymen must keep silent about the injustices that cry for remedy and the evils that infest our society, or that they must look with callous unconcern upon human suffering and remain indifferent to crucial national and international problems. To do so is to repudiate an integral part of Christian responsibility and to run the risk of severing two vital aspects of the Christian life that God has joined together — namely, faith and works. Therefore, to deny or repudiate Christian social concern and participation in public affairs not only severs what God has indissolubly united but also thwarts the divinely willed purpose of our regeneration as children of God. It is significant that such great New Testament epistles as Romans, Galatians, Ephesians, Colossians, and Hebrews begin with saving doctrine and end with the obligation to practice it.

Acceptance of civic responsibility; loyal participation in government (including the duty of speaking out against policies that seem wrong); personal and self-sacrificial action in behalf of the oppressed and underprivileged, the sick and helpless, regardless of color, nationality, or creed — these, while not the Gospel, are the inescapable outcome of the Gospel and thus part of the Christian vocation binding upon clergy and laity alike. In the incomparable words of Christ, "Inasmuch as ye have done it unto one of the least of these my brethren, ye have done it unto me" (Matt. 25:40).

The principle that the Church may not enter into politics does not mean that either the individual churches or their ministers and members may remain comfortably aloof from injustice and remote from human oppression and suffering. The calling of the Church is indeed spiritual. Its primary obligation is to proclaim the great Good News of salvation through Jesus Christ. It must be utterly convinced that the ultimate solution to the problem of humanity is regeneration by the Holy Spirit.

For evangelicals these things are not debatable. Yet they are accompanied by some corollaries. Chief among these is the principle that not all proclamation of the Gospel is verbal. Deeds of compassion done in Christ's name also make him known and open the door for him to do his saving work.

It may well be that some evangelicals need to learn that social work is not necessarily sub-Christian; that, for a believer, public service and politics may be a God-given vocation; that civil rights is a moral problem; that Christian youth may be called to the Peace Corps; that teaching retarded children may be as Christ-like a calling as leading a class in child evangelism. Witnessing is not a disembodied activity. When clothed with deeds of mercy, it may become fully as effective as when dressed in the attire of the pulpit.

The Old Testament prophets were deeply involved in public affairs. In burning words they spoke out against the injustices of their day. Yet they were not remiss in pointing to the coming Messiah, who would save his people from their sins. The God who inspired them guarded their ministry against imbalance. Our Lord Jesus Christ came to seek and to save that which was lost and to give his life a ransom for many. Yet his teaching and activity were also directed toward other human need. The apostles preached the Gospel and also ministered to individuals, as have God's servants in every age. And if this is a time for evangelicals to reconsider their responsibility for social concern and public affairs, let them do so according to the biblical pattern.

— *Christianity Today,* January 17, 1964

Eleven
CHRISTIAN COMPASSION

To be insensitive to the needs of others is for Christians a denial
of who they are and of what their Lord requires of them. If
the main theme of Scripture is redemption, united to it as effect
to cause is the theme of responsibility for one's neighbor. From
the question in Genesis 4, "Am I my brother's keeper?," through
the epistles, the Bible demands concern for the well-being of
others.

Woven into the very fabric of Christianity is compassion. At
the beginning of his ministry, Jesus applied to himself the
words of Isaiah, "The Spirit of the Lord is upon me, because
he has anointed me to preach good news to the poor. He has
sent me to proclaim release to the captives and recovering of
sight to the blind, to set at liberty those who are oppressed, to
proclaim the acceptable year of the Lord." At the heart of Jesus'
ministry was concern for the individual. He left the ninety and
nine and sought the one. For him the individual had immeasurable worth; he died not for an impersonal mass of humanity
but for persons.

Paul's exhortation, "Have this mind among yourselves, which
you have in Christ Jesus," points to the supreme example of
unselfishness who laid aside "the insignia of his divine majesty"
and became obedient unto death. Our Lord's word to his
disciples, "If any man would come after me, let him deny himself and take up his cross and follow me," demands selfless
living. Moreover, Christ spoke in terms of his own identification
with the deprived and underprivileged: "I was a stranger and
you welcomed me, I was naked and you clothed me, I was sick
and you visited me, I was in prison and you came to me.....
Truly, I say to you, as you did it to one of the least of these my
brethren, you did it to me...as you did it not to one of the

least of these, you did it not to me." Involvement in the lives of others is an essential element of Christian compassion. To cherish one's own rights without willingness to be personally involved in the need and deprivation of others is a kind of negative testimony that keeps those from listening to the Gospel who need it most. If the world feels that we who stand for doctrinal purity lack compassion for the wounds of the world, it will pay little attention to what we say.

Distortion of truth is always dangerous. Half-truths are never less than deceptive. Evangelicals justly criticize the social gospel as a half-truth. There is only one Gospel, and that is the Good News of salvation through the death and resurrection of Jesus Christ. Those who insist upon this do not deny the social aspect of Christianity. They simply take their stand with the apostle who warned the Galatians so vehemently against any other gospel than that which he had taught them. To refuse to allow the social gospel to supplant *the* Gospel does not cancel the command of God for Christians to help those in need.

Evangelicals also may fall into the snare of the half-truth in respect to the practice of Christian compassion. Whereas liberalism has tended to substitute for the Gospel itself the compassionate result of the Gospel, some evangelicals have tended to evade that result by resorting to another kind of half-truth. Thus there are some whose lack of concern for social justice is reflected in an uncritical use of the statement, "You can't legislate morality."

Now there is a sense in which it is indeed true that you cannot legislate personal morality. Yet it is also true that the tranquillity of society demands legislation for crimes against humanity and the state. Webster defines law as "rules of conduct enforced by a controlling authority." When President Lincoln signed the Emancipation Proclamation and when the Thirteenth Amendment was adopted, there were those who defended slavery as morally permissible. Now, however, not even in areas most deeply committed to segregation would human slavery be defended. Measures designed to protect the individual helped change the climate of moral opinion about an evil that had already been on the conscience of many.

World Leprosy Sunday is at hand. Compassion for millions of fellow human beings afflicted by this dread disease is not debatable. Christ said, "Cleanse the leper." There are very few lepers in the United States, and these few are well cared for. Most lepers are on the other side of the globe, eight to ten thousand miles away from this favored land. They must have our generous help. Yet a nearer test of Christian compassion relates to the problems on our doorsteps. To minister to lepers abroad, or to others in Africa, Asia, and the isles of the sea, while essential, will not fulfill our obligation to bind up wounds of the needy in our midst.

Without departing from the zeal for the Gospel which is one of the glories of evangelicalism, we need to recover the realism with which our Lord spoke of discipleship. His teaching bristles with hard sayings. He spoke about seeking first not material prosperity but the Kingdom of God and his righteousness. He called the man who gave priority to things and based his life upon them a fool. He said that whoever would lose his life for his sake would find it and whoever would save his life would lose it. He called believers "the salt of the earth" and expected them to have an ameliorating effect upon the society in which they lived. He said, "If you love me, you will keep my commandments."

God sent his Son to proclaim the Gospel. Therefore we must proclaim it. God sent him to do works of love and mercy. Therefore we must do works of love and mercy. God sent him to the Cross. Therefore our lives must bear the marks of the Cross. To witness to the saving truth in Christ is the obligation of all believers. But it is not their only obligation. One of Jesus' most poignant sayings is the question, "Why do you call me 'Lord, Lord,' and not do what I tell you?"

Christian compassion is a matter of the heart. Yet it is more than emotion. It is the expression of full commitment of all we have and are to the Lord who gave himself for us. Christian compassion is love in action on behalf of others. To the extent that it is not manifest in the believer's life, the believer has failed his Lord in not keeping the first and great commandment and the second, which is like unto it. Failure in compassion betokens an inadequate view of the very heart of Christianity, which is Christ's self-giving for a lost world. "By this we know love," said the beloved disciple, "that he laid down his life for us; and we ought to lay down our lives for the brethren. But if any one has this world's goods and sees his brother in need, yet closes his heart against him, how does God's love abide in him?" John is speaking within the Christian community, but our Lord's parable of the Good Samaritan warrants the widest application of his words.

When all of evangelicalism learns to match its zeal for the proclamation of the Gospel and its shining record of good works abroad with active compassion for the alleviation of injustice and human deprivation at home, it will move forward in a resurgence of power. Those who proclaim sound doctrine cannot escape the test of reality. Evangelicalism is not exempt from Jesus' criterion, "By their fruits you shall know them." Not all fundamentals are doctrinal. If the fundamental of compassion has sometimes been lacking in evangelical life and practice, let it be restored, even though to restore it may be costly.

— *Christianity Today*, January 20, 1965

Twelve
CIVIL RIGHTS
AND CHRISTIAN CONCERN

History will evaluate 1964 with its decision on the civil rights bill as one of the critical years in our national annals. The issue now before the country is more than one of integration versus segregation; it has to do with the integrity of our democracy.

As the Senate debate moves toward the day of decision, one senses a feeling of inevitability. This is a time of hard choices, not just for the senators who must cast their votes but also for the rank and file of their fellow Americans. We are all involved. The hour is long past — if it ever was at hand — when a man or woman might stand and watch the civil rights struggle as from a window overlooking the busy street.

What is happening this spring in the Senate is not an academic debate in which one listens to affirmative, negative, and rebuttal, and then awaits the judges' decision. No American, and least of all a Christian American, has the right to follow the civil rights debate unconcerned and unmoved. The vote on H.R. 7152 will indelibly affect the nation's future.

Patriotism demands individual concern in a matter so close to the public welfare. And patriotism is neither sub-Christian nor outmoded, even in this sophisticated age. For Christians it is plainly enjoined in Scripture. Moreover, ethics are united with patriotism; no Christian can stand passively by when the good of others is jeopardized. Obedience to the law of love for one's neighbor requires concern for the welfare of one's neighbor.

The kind of civil rights bill the nation will have depends in the first instance upon how the Senate votes. But it is equally true that how the Senate votes will reflect public opinion. In fact, the extra weight that will tip the balance one way or the other will come from the people. As James Reston, the well-known Washington correspondent, has said, "In the end, the temper of the country is likely to decide the issue."

What, then, are some guidelines for Christian concern regarding this great question? Four in particular may be listed: (1) the necessity for informed opinion; (2) the right of all Americans to equal rights of citizenship; (3) the obligation to respect those whose conscience leads them to convictions different from one's own; (4) the recognition that, essential as legislation is, moral problems are ultimately solved not by passing laws but by changing hearts.

First, informed opinion is demanded of every Christian who is in earnest about fulfilling his civic responsibilities. Valid opinion cannot be derived from ignorance nor developed out of a fog of second-hand ideas. With an issue so important as civil rights, it is not enough to let others do one's thinking or to reach conclusions based largely upon emotion.

If, as has already been stated, the climate of opinion will tip the balance in civil rights legislation, Christians to whom the moral aspects of the question must be paramount will have to take time and trouble to inform themselves about the issues at stake. This not only means reading what Senator X or Senator Y declares, what commentator A or pundit B writes, or what this newspaper or that news magazine says; it also means being familiar with the bill itself so as to know what its provisions are. Then, knowing what is involved, a Christian is obligated to come to his own conclusions thoughtfully and prayerfully. Only so does he earn, as it were, the right to add his weight to the growing amount of influence that is bound to affect the voting in the Senate.

Second, there is a major premise on which concerned opinion must rest. That premise is the constitutional right of all Americans to full citizenship. In particular, this means that no American should, because of his color, be deprived of his right to vote, rest, eat, sleep, be educated, live, and work on the same basis as other citizens. Anything short of this is an intolerable deprivation of rights for one segment of the population, a deprivation that, by reason of its inherent injustice, violates basic morality.

Third, there is the obligation to respect the conscience of those who differ with their fellow Americans and fellow Christians regarding constitutional aspects of the legislation under consideration. The civil rights question is more than a controversy: it is a great conflict. In a conflict of such dimensions there are divergent convictions. Surely it is no compromise to recognize that however wrong one's neighbor may appear to be, he may be sincerely and honestly wrong.

Therefore, to dechristianize those who disagree with certain aspects of the civil rights bill is incompatible with Christian love and tolerance. Moreover, to equate any particular position regarding the bill with the Gospel of Jesus Christ may come perilously close to the Galatian heresy of proclaiming "another gospel." While justice for all, regardless of race, is an inescapable outcome of the Gospel, it is not itself the Gospel any more than any other fulfillment of the law of love is the Gospel. Let race prejudice and hatred be unmasked as the sin they surely are (and in the North as well as the South who is wholly free from them?) ; but let not a stand for civil justice or participation in demonstrations be confused with the Gospel through which alone men are redeemed by faith.

Fourth, there is the principle that law of itself, essential though it is, can be only a proximate, not the ultimate, solution of the deep problems of society. For the maintenance of the structure of society and the control of evil, laws are essential. Yet it may be that one of our national failings is the misconception that once a law is passed, a problem is forever settled. But laws must be obeyed, and ultimate obedience is a matter of the heart, not of compulsion, necessary though enforcement is. Sin is common to all, regardless of color. Therefore, Christian concern demands the ceaseless proclamation of the Gospel as the ground of ultimate reconciliation of the racial revolution.

There are also other matters of concern. While the Church should not engage in politics, as many evangelicals hold, it is nevertheless an inescapable obligation for Christians to take part in public affairs. Historically, amelioration of social problems has come through men and women whose hearts and consciences God has touched. The classical evangelical position is that the

Gospel must be preached and that those whom Christ has redeemed will go out and serve as he leads them. If some Christians feel it their duty as individuals to stand side by side with their Negro brethren in the struggle, who is to say them nay? Are they not free to exercise their right of protest just as their more socially conservative brethren are free to respond in their way to the racial question? Yet granting this, it must also be said that restraint in demonstrations and respect for law are urgently needed; extremism and threats of violence will only impede the processes of legislation.

But what of the civil rights bill? Constitutional aspects of the methods of enforcement specified in it require safeguards against possible misuse of the great powers conferred. Thus the position of some that the bill must be passed without the alteration of a word is unwise. At certain points it should and probably will be amended. But the need for legislation exists.

Christians may differ about the civil rights bill. Yet the path of Christian responsibility is plain. It leads inevitably to a position worked out before God. And that position ought to be made known. If individuals ask, "What can I do?" let them voice their convictions to their senators now, and in these troubled days pray for the Senate and all in places of leadership.

Evangelicals, and indeed the Church as a whole, have lagged in racial relations. Especially has segregation within the churches been a stumbling block. Had the Church really practiced the love and brotherhood it preaches, the present crisis might have been averted.

These failures have indeed been lamentable. But once they are confessed, they must be put aside and attention centered upon the needs and obligations of the present. In this time of decision, evangelical spectatorism must give way to evangelical action that supports, as conscience leads, such legislation as assures all citizens the freedoms guaranteed them in the Constitution.

— *Christianity Today,* May 8, 1964

Thirteen

CIGARETTES
AND THE STEWARDSHIP OF THE BODY

Great works of literature, art, and music, the beauty of nature, friendship and true love are enhanced by close association. But there are other things, familiarity with which tends to breed unconcern if not actual contempt. Groups as well as individuals may become so used to situations that are wrong or dangerous as not to see them as they are. Thus American society tolerates certain things that are exacting an enormous toll in suffering and life. Among these are the devastation on the highways to the extent last year of about 40,000 deaths plus many more injuries; the five million alcoholics with the accumulated tragedy; and the 40,000 deaths from lung cancer in 1962, largely traceable, according to the American Cancer Society, to cigarette smoking.

Long familiarity with these social phenomena has produced among us callous unconcern for the human welfare they jeopardize. When areas stricken by natural disaster need aid or when our imagination is captured by the plight of miners trapped underground, we are capable of showing great "reverence for life." Yet at the same time we continue strangely apathetic to much needless suffering and loss of life right on our doorstep.

Consider, for example, the relationship of cigarettes to lung cancer. *The Consumers Union Report on Smoking and the Public Interest* presents the problem with thoroughness and with an abundance of statistical and experimental evidence. As the subtitle of the first chapter of the report says, "we are living in an epidemic"—an epidemic of lung cancer. This is plain fact. And in the light of it the unchanged determination of the cigarette industry to sell to as many people as possible a product that is a leading cause of this epidemic is dismaying. One is astonished to read that cigarette sales in 1962 amounted to one half trillion, thus exceeding by about one hundred billion the total sales in 1953, when the country was first informed on a wide scale of the medical evidence relating cigarette smoke to cancer of the lung. Moreover, when one also learns that the cigarette industry last year spent over $200 million on advertising, a sum representing an increase of 134 per cent over a ten-year period during which evidence of the cigarette-cancer relation has piled up, dismay and astonishment give way to indignation.

We urge upon all with a concern for the public welfare a careful reading of the Consumers Union report. After the chapters setting forth medical evidence, the section in which the authors analyze the attitude of the industry reveals a determined refusal to face facts and a promotional cynicism that, while economically understandable, are indefensible. If, as the report more than once says, "1,000,000 children now of school age may die prematurely of lung cancer" (and the statistic is well founded), this alone shows that we have a social and moral problem that demands action, such as has already been taken in one way or another by the governments of Great Britain, Italy, Denmark, Sweden, and Finland. Of these, Great Britain, despite its stake of £900 million (about $2.5 billion) in tobacco excise taxes, has mounted the fullest offensive against cigarettes with a broad and intense program of traveling exhibits, posters, films, and advertising.

The Consumers Union Report on Smoking and the Public Interest approaches the problem on a medical and social basis without direct reference to its moral aspect, although ethical implications inevitably shine through its discussion of the industry's deliberate blindness to evidence and the mendacity of its advertising. But the Christian community is in a different position. It can no more look at the cigarette-lung cancer problem from a morally neutral point of view than it can be oblivious of the moral implications of the daily slaughter on the highways and the human wreckage through alcoholism.

So the question arises, "Is there a Christian position in relation to the cigarette problem?" We believe that there is indeed such a position and that it is a clear and biblical one. Prior to

1953, when evidence about the carcinogens in cigarette smoke began to be widely publicized, the Christian attitude toward cigarettes was different from what it is today. Then some Christian groups equated smoking with worldliness and ruled it out on the ground of incompatibility with "a separated life." Others, including many fully committed to the evangelical faith, considered cigarettes along with other forms of smoking an optional practice to be decided through the exercise of Christian liberty. There was also the point of view, cutting across both groups, that frowned on smoking as a physically harmful habit, although clear evidence of its link to lung cancer had not been found.

Today the situation is radically different. Abundant evidence has accumulated to implicate cigarette smoke in lung cancer as well as in coronary heart disease and emphysema. Apart from quibbles whether it is the cause of lung cancer, statistically and experimentally it is unmistakably related to the current epidemic of that disease. The degree of this relationship is high. Dr. Alton Ochsner, an authority on lung cancer and president in 1962 of the International College of Surgeons, does not hesitate to express it like this: "I have made the statement, and I am sure it is true, that every person who smokes cigarettes will develop cancer of the lung if he lives long enough. The only thing that will ever keep him from such cancer is that he will die of something else before he develops it" ("Dabblers in Death," *The Sunday School Times,* June 22, 1963).

It may well be that habitual cigarette smoking is no longer for the Christian a mere take-it-or-leave-it matter. It has moved from an optional indulgence to a question of the stewardship of the body. For there *is* a stewardship of the body. On the scriptural ground that the God who gives us our bodies requires accountability for their use, none of us has the right to contract any habit that has been shown to lead to grave illness and premature death. Because the body of the believer is, as the Apostle Paul tells us, "the temple of the Holy Spirit" (I Cor. 6:19), no Christian has the right to destroy it through cigarette addiction, even though the addiction be socially acceptable. Nor, it should also be said, has he the right to destroy it through

81

any other practice, whether addiction to alcohol or habitual indulgence in overeating.

This principle of the stewardship of the body has a biblical corollary — namely, regard for the weaker brother. Paul said it drastically, ". . . judge this rather, that no man put a stumbling-block or an occasion to fall in his brother's way. . . . Destroy not him with thy meat, for whom Christ died" (Rom. 14:13, 15). Responsibility for the effect of personal practices on others is, as Oscar Cullmann has pointed out, set in a redemptive context — "him . . . for whom Christ died."

In recent years the age at which young people (who may validly be considered our weaker brethren) begin to smoke cigarettes has fallen. According to a study of New York teen-agers made by the American Cancer Society, 9 per cent of the school children from twelve to fourteen years old who were questioned were smoking daily, and by the tenth grade 40 per cent of the boys were smoking "just about every day" (*The New York Times,* October 13, 1963). As the American Public Health Association declared in its statement of 1959 (quoted in *The Consumers Union Report,* p. 10), "If present trends continue, lung cancer will claim the lives of more than 1,000,000 present school children in this country before they reach the age of 70 years."

Every experienced teacher of adolescents knows that a major motivation of teen-age youth is the desire for grown-up status. Like driving a car, cigarette smoking is a status symbol; but it is much more accessible and ultimately far more hazardous than driving. If the habit were not so prevalent among adults and if it were not so continually promoted through advertising cleverly linking it with manly prowess, beauty, and sex, it would lose much of its fascination for youth.

Cigarettes are not only physiologically dangerous; their addictive property also cannot be overlooked. It is this factor that explains in part the paradox of their continued use. Dr. Charles S. Cameron, medical and scientific director of the American Cancer Society, referred obliquely to the addictive factor in these words: "If the degree of association which has been established between cancer of the lung and smoking were shown to exist between cancer of the lung, and say, eating spinach, no one would raise a hand against the proscription of spinach from the national diet" ("What We Know About Smoking and Lung Cancer," *The Atlantic Monthly,* January, 1956).

For both youth and adults the habitual use of cigarettes is incompatible with the biblical principle of the stewardship of the body. For Christian adults in particular it contributes by force of example to teen-age addiction to a dangerous and often fatal habit and thus violates the biblical principle of responsibility for one's brother. No longer may it be considered a harmless, optional practice to be taken up merely for personal gratification.

— *Christianity Today,* November 8, 1963

Fourteen

ABSTINENCE MAKES SENSE

Three acute problems relating to the public welfare — automobile accidents, cigarette smoking, and alcoholism — are exacting an enormous toll in human suffering. Of them, alcoholism is the oldest, the most complex, and in its effects the most far-reaching with a national total of more than five million alcoholics, a number that is increasing at the rate of 200,000 each year. Moreover, 25 million others — families and friends of alcoholics — are affected; and the problem also reaches extensively into such areas as crime and accidents.

What man does with drink has been a problem since the dawn of history. Compared with it, cigarette smoking and the misuse of automobiles are the most recent of newcomers. Yet apart from obvious dissimilarities, there is a kinship among the three problems in that each is to some extent controllable by human volition. And wherever human suffering is preventable or controllable, there Christian concern must be manifest.

According to the American Medical Association and the World Health Organization, alcoholism is a disease. (From a purely medical standpoint this is true; but the Bible speaks too emphatically of drunkenness as sin to relieve alcoholics of all moral responsibility.) Yet the etiology and exact nature of this disease are still imperfectly known, as Dr. E. M. Jellinek's study, *The Disease Concept of Alcoholism,* shows. The strange paradox is that hundreds of millions of dollars are spent annually to persuade people to run the risk of contracting a devastating malady that ruins personality and shortens by an average of twelve years the life-span of those who have it. The decision of WQXR, the radio station of *The New York Times,* to accept advertising of hard liquor in violation of the code of the National Association of Broadcasters points to the need for more active government concern with the present state of advertising of alcoholic beverages.

It may be that alcohol has so long been surrounded by an aura of social respectability that it has truly become what Dr. Jellinek calls "the domesticated drug." But its domestication has not mitigated its dangers. And because its use is so intimately related to social customs, attitudes toward alcohol are all-important. Christians differ about its use, and the Bible does not condemn all drinking. Thus problems relating to it must be considered both with care and with charity.

Nevertheless, the plain facts about alcoholism need to be faced. Whether or not one thinks drinking permissible, 75 million Americans *are* using alcoholic beverages and one out of fifteen of these drinkers is suffering from alcoholism. Thus the United States with its multitudes of alcoholics shares with France the leadership of the world in the incidence of this malady. Teen-age drinking is soaring. According to the National Safety Council, special studies have indicated that in fatal highway accidents as many as half of the victims had been drinking. The annual cost of alcoholism to our society is well over $1 billion, and the yearly expenditure of $12 billion for intoxicating beverages far exceeds what is given the churches of the nation. Other statistics implicating alcohol in mental and physical diseases of various kinds and showing the enormous loss to business and industry occasioned by problem drinkers are well known.

The foregoing stands as essential background for reconsideration of a solution that has long been known and practiced by a significant minority and yet is strangely slighted in many current discussions of alcohol and its perils. That solution is voluntary abstinence.

With all that is being written about alcoholism and with the sociological, medical, physiological, and psychological research being devoted to its cause and cure, there is no secret whatever about a sure method of preventing it. No one who does not drink will ever become an alcoholic. Moreover, those who do not drink, while not exempt from highway accidents, will not be subject to accidents resulting from impairment of their own faculties by even very small amounts of alcohol in the body.

Surely the time has come for a careful, persistent, and persuasive presentation of the fact that abstinence makes sense. Regardless of differing religious traditions and varying interpretations of what Scripture says about drinking, youth today — and they are the future drinkers of tomorrow — have the right to hear the plain case for abstinence as a valid and socially acceptable answer to the alcohol problem. Unfortunately this answer is not being given as widely as it should be in literature about alcohol. Too often the gratuitous assumption is made that youth are bound to drink anyway and that therefore they need only to be taught how to drink and how to diagnose signs of trouble in their drinking. One wonders whether this attitude is indicative of adult reluctance to set forth a solution many have themselves rejected and whether it may reflect a covert hostility of the drinker to the non-drinker.

Quite apart from the biblical argument that rests upon consideration for one's weaker brother, there are compelling reasons why abstinence is a valid answer to the question (To drink or not to drink?) with which our society confronts youth today.

What, then, are these reasons? They are related to an enormously significant fact about alcohol and its use. *There is no way of knowing who among any group that begins to drink will become an alcoholic; no medical or psychological research can accurately predict the victims of alcoholism.* Estimating conservatively the number of American drinkers as 75 million and dividing a similarly conservative estimate of 5 million alcoholics into this number, the chance of a beginning drinker's becoming an alcoholic is at least one in fifteen.

Someone has put it this way. Suppose a man goes to an airline counter to book a flight. The ticket is purchased, and the attendant delivers it with these words: "You should know, sir, that on this plane, seating seventy-five passengers, five seats at some time during the flight will suddenly give way and drop their occupants out of the plane." The purchaser replies, "Don't put me in one of those seats." "But," says the attendant, "that's impossible; we don't know the seats that will give way. Have a good flight, sir."

Youth need to be told that drinking is a gamble and that the stakes are high — not indeed instant calamity, as in the illustration, but personal disaster that might involve loss of work, marriage, children, friends, self-respect, and, if not checked, life itself. (Remission is possible, but only in about 50 per cent of the cases.)

This is the risk against which the oft-heard advantages of alcohol as a social lubricant, a means for relaxing tension, an aid to gracious living, and a compliance with prevalent custom, must be weighed. For there is no way of choosing these without running the unavoidable risk of being the one out of fifteen to become an alcoholic. Let youth be told this plainly, factually, and emphatically. Along with this, let them be told also that they are going to live in a society that wants them to drink with it and that will make every effort by social pressure and the unremitting impact of advertising to get them to drink with it.

Nothing short of this is fair to youth. Theirs is the hazard, and they must be informed. The reasonableness of abstinence rests on considerations of responsibility, example to others, and the danger of alcohol itself. Many of those who advocate abstinence find their warrant in Paul's words, "All things are lawful unto me, but all things are not expedient..." (I Cor. 6:12; 10:23), and in his principle of restricting one's liberty in consideration of the weaker brother: "It is good neither ... to drink wine, nor any thing whereby thy brother stumbleth, or is offended, or is made weak" (Rom. 14:21).

Abstinence can only be voluntary. Enforced group abstinence cannot succeed. Nevertheless, to refrain from a practice so fraught with danger and to do so not only for self but also for the sake of others is a true Christian answer to one of the great social problems of our time. Consequently it must be presented unashamedly and unequivocally.

In other periods, such as Bible times, the problems about alcohol were different from today. But these are not Bible times. The stresses of living in this space age make the human organism more susceptible to the perils of alcohol than in ancient Palestine. The driver of an oxcart or the traveler by horse or donkey faced different demands for instant decision than the man at the wheel of over a ton of metal propelled by a multi-horsepower engine. God expects of us the adjustment of maturity to current problems and holds us responsible for indulgences that may imperil our own lives and the lives of others. In a day like this, voluntary abstinence to the glory of God and for the sake of others is a reasonable and safe solution to the problem of alcohol. It requires the courage of conviction. Let individual Christians earnestly consider it for themselves. And let parents, schools, and churches examine their obligation to teach their youth that abstinence makes sense.

— *Christianity Today,* April 24, 1964

CULTURE AND TASTE

Fifteen
THE CHRISTIAN'S INTELLECTUAL LIFE

The chief business of a college has to do with the thinking of its students. God created man to be a thinking being. The Bible recognizes the central importance of thought. It does not, of course, speak in terms of modern psychology. When it deals with man's most characteristic activity, it uses not only the word "mind" but also more often words like "heart" and "soul." It tells us that we are made in the image of the only wise God, an image that, though ruined through the fall beyond our power to repair, is not beyond God's power to regenerate through the work of Christ.

In the Bible the thought life is decisive. Solomon says, "As [a man] thinketh in his heart, so is he." And again, "Keep thy heart with all diligence; for out of it are the issues of life." Paul exhorts us not to be conformed to this world but to be transformed by the renewing of our minds; and he gives us the charter for Christian thought when he says: "Finally, brethren, whatsoever things are true, whatsoever things are honest, whatsoever things are just, whatsoever things are pure, whatsoever things are lovely, whatsoever things are of good report; if there be any virtue, and if there be any praise, think on these things" (Phil. 4:8).

Blaise Pascal, certainly one of the most biblical of all the great scientists and philosophers, says in his *Pensées*, "Man is but a reed, the most feeble thing in nature; but he is a thinking reed. . . . Let us endeavour, then, to think well." In other words, one of the great marks of man's uniqueness is his God-given capacity to think. Consequently, anything that diminishes our thinking tends to dehumanize us through making us less than what God created us to be.

We ought, therefore, as partners in Christian education, to

91

take seriously our obligation to live our intellectual life to the glory of God. For us who receive the Bible as the Word of God, who ourselves know the power of the Saviour who died and rose for us, the Christian's intellectual life is not an optional matter. It is for all of us. It is a "must" for every believing student and teacher.

The Christian call to the intellectual life is not just to an elite, a chosen few. It is not merely for members of the scholastic honor society, or for the faculty. Said Sir William Ramsay, "Christianity is the religion of an educated mind." Observe that he did not say that it is the religion of a brilliant or a gifted mind. We are not responsible for the extent of our native intelligence but for the extent of our use of the ability God has given us. And in the Christian liberal arts college the talents of the mind must be developed into Christian intellect. There is, as Professor Jacques Barzun of Columbia shows in *The House of Intellect,* a crucial distinction between intelligence and intellectualism; the former is our native endowment in mental aptitude, while the latter is the use we make of our individual ability in helping to develop a cultural tradition.

So let us go on to see some of the implications of the development of Christian intellect. Consider its distinctive nature. We Christians are people of the Book, not just any book, but the Bible — the greatest, most beautiful, most profound Book in the world, on the truths of which the Christian college rests. Because this Book has to do with man in the entirety of his being, and because of our relationship to the living Lord who is made known to us through it, our intellectual life is much bigger than our reason alone. It embraces all of us, including our will and our emotions. Man is a unit; we cannot isolate and compartmentalize our faculties. As Dr. A. W. Tozer put it: "The Greek church father, Nicephorus, taught that we should learn to think with our heart. 'Force your mind to descend into the heart,' he says, 'and to remain there. . . .' When you thus enter into the place of the heart . . . it will teach you things which in no other way you will ever learn."

Look now at the scope of the Christian's intellectual life. The charge is often made that those of us who take the Word of

God as our guide are bound to be restricted in outlook. To this the best answer is to turn back to Philippians 4:8 where Paul outlines the scope of our thought and urges us to "think on" (literally "ponder," "let your mind dwell on") six categories of things: those things that are "true," "honest" (honorable), "just" (according to God's requirements), "pure" (and remember that purity of thought comes from purity of soul), "lovely" (all that is beautiful), and "of good report" (before God and our fellow man). What horizons these six open up! They invite Christian thought to explore every aspect of truth to the glory of God.

Yet we must remember that our pursuit of truth entails an obligation of personal commitment. Just as we should say with Paul, "For me to live is Christ," so we must, as A. P. Sertillanges suggests, learn to say in every aspect of our intellectual life, "For me to live is truth"; for Christ is himself the truth. As he is revealed in his perfection in the Word, he is the ultimate criterion and measure of truth.

Now to live for the truth means to adopt a scale of values different from that which surrounds us. It was Archbishop William Temple who remarked, "The world, as we live in it, is like a shop window where some mischievous person has broken in the night to change all the price labels, so that the cheap things have the higher price on them and the really precious things are marked down." Why is there this twisting, this reversal of values in the world? One reason is the divorce in worldly thinking between truth and its ethical and spiritual implications.

One of the contributions of Christian thought to our times must be the recovery of the ethical and spiritual dimensions of truth. No matter how great the prestige of a college or university, the search for truth merely on the level of the reason will not do. To hold truth in a moral and spiritual vacuum is not good enough. Thoughtful secular educators are beginning to see this. Witness these words of President John Sloan Dickey of Dartmouth College: "I believe we must at least redouble our effort to restore the relevancy of moral purpose as an essential companion of intellectual purpose and power

93

in any learning that presumes to liberate a man.... There is simply no civilized alternative to having personal power answerable to conscience."

What Dr. Dickey and others like him are seeking — that is, the connection between intellectual and moral purpose — is at the center of our Christian heritage. Observe that Paul's pattern of the subject matter of our thought — the things that are "true," "honorable," "just," "pure," "lovely," and "of good report"— is united throughout with ethical values.

But the Christian's intellectual life goes even deeper than this union with morality. It is at bottom a life of faith. Let us never make the mistake of thinking that faith is unrelated to knowledge and the development of intellect. In the deepest sense, believing is the door to knowledge.

The blind spot in the striving of the non-Christian mind for intellectual achievement lies in the incorrigible secularism with which it disregards faith. Secularism is, as someone has defined it, the practice of the absence of God. If it is our privilege as Christians to see where the world is blind, let us be very humble about it. Let us also be very sure that our intellectual life is infused with faith. For only the thinker who "believes that God is and that he is a rewarder of them that diligently seek him" uses his mind, as he ought, to God's glory.

The challenge of the Christian intellectual life is indeed great. But it is not an easy challenge. It costs to have a mind that is really dedicated to the Lord. The reason why there are Christians who are not going on intellectually to the glory of God is not that they are dull or incapable of learning, but simply that they will not pay the price. And the price will not come down. It is nothing less than the discipline of self-restraint and plain hard work.

Dr. Allan Heely, distinguished headmaster of the Lawrenceville School, was once asked by a voluble lady, enamored of progressive education, this question: "What, Dr. Heely, is your idea of the ideal curriculum for growing boys?" He replied as follows: "Any program of worth-while studies so long as all of it is hard and some of it is unpleasant." This was a severe but wholesome answer which applies in principle to the whole range of education on through graduate school. A great fault of education today is that much of it is too easy, and the fault applies to college as well as to grade school. No student will ever make sound progress in learning if he chooses courses merely because he thinks they will be easy. No Christian, however pious, will ever grow intellectually if he feeds his mind on trash, on the third-rate; if he never on his own reads some hard books, listens to some great and profound music, or tries to converse seriously about difficult subjects.

Turning from these things to the greatest Book of all, let me ask, What is the place of the Bible in our lives? Have we the fortitude to maintain inviolate a daily time alone with the Word of God? One may be an intellectual person without the Bible, but one will never be a Christian intellectual without it.

Finally, we grow in intellect in the broadest and deepest sense as we submit ourselves to our teacher. And who is that? As Bishop Stephen F. Bayne, Jr., said in a semicentennial address at the Kent School, "God Is the Teacher." In the Christian college — and herein lies the inestimable value of a committed Christian college — the living God is recognized as the source of all wisdom and excellence. And how does he teach? Let me say it reverently. God is not a progressive educator. He teaches us daily, as we pay the price of hard thinking. He teaches us through his Word. He teaches us through teachers who in turn are taught by him. He teaches us through the discipline of trial and disappointment and suffering, and through our successes too. But most of all he teaches us through our Lord Jesus Christ. When God teaches us, he is always saying in and through and above whatever we are studying and learning for ourselves, or, in the case of us teachers, what we are teaching others, "This is my beloved Son; hear him."

The intellectual life at its highest and best is above all else a Christ-centered life. It means having the mind of the Lord Jesus. It has a goal, the magnificent, lofty goal, as Paul said, of "bringing into captivity every thought to the obedience of Christ."

Like the high priest of Israel who had written on the mitre over his forehead, "Holiness unto the Lord," so the Christian student and scholar, dedicated to the intellectual life, must have written over his mind, "Holiness unto the Lord," as he seeks to ponder and dwell on the truth.

Convocation address at Houghton College, 1960.
— *Christianity Today,* May 8, 1961

Sixteen
THE IDEA OF EXCELLENCE
AND OUR OBLIGATION TO IT

Educators have an innate fondness for slogans. "Educating the Whole Child"; "Educating for Life Adjustment"; "Educating for One World"; "Educating for the Space Age." So the slogans come and go. Most of them have had a real point to make, and our schools have doubtless been helped by considering them. All of them have faced the danger of wearing out into clichés. But excellence, the pursuit and practice of the best in teaching, this surely is a theme that we ought not let slip like the slogans of yesterday.

Let us, therefore, take a close look at "The Idea of Excellence." What is it? By what criterion do we determine the excellent, yes, even the more excellent, in our study and in our teaching? It is strange that in all the discussion regarding excellence, so little is said about the idea itself. Albert Einstein once remarked that we live in an age of perfect means and confused goals. This confusion relates to some extent to our thinking regarding excellence.

We all take for granted that there is such a thing. Like a shining thread it runs through educational thought from Plato, who defined education as the "training in excellence from youth upwards which makes a man passionately desire to be a perfect citizen and teaches him how to rule with justice," to John Gardner's recent book, entitled *Excellence.*

The fact is that the idea of excellence is a bit like the Greek god Proteus, who had, you will recall, the ability, when grasped, of changing into another form. John Gardner compares the word "excellence" to the Rorshach ink blot test in which each individual sees something different. And it is true that what each of us sees in the idea of excellence reveals much about him.

"But," someone persists, "what *is* excellence?" Well, the dictionary uses terms like these: "first-rate," "superior," "extremely good of its kind." In doing so it underscores something as important as it is obvious. Excellence is a comparative term.

As the first-rate, excellence stands over against the second-rate; as the best, it contrasts with the good or the better. If the idea is protean, it is because of the varying standards and differing points of view by which we judge it. Are we, then, forever shut up to relativism in respect to excellence? Are there no ultimates in the light of which our reaching for it may be assessed?

There is, I believe, an ultimate point of reference for the things that are excellent. We are not shut up to relativism. This becomes clear as we turn from the dictionary and from most educational writing to another source — namely, the biblical view of excellence.

Here is an idea of excellence that points away from us. It directs our gaze upwards and outside ourselves. Implicit in the biblical concept of excellence is the idea of transcendence. The words used have such root meanings as "height," "loftiness," and "majesty." In Scripture, ultimate excellence is seen as belonging not to men but to God, as in the description of him in Deuteronomy as the One "who rideth . . . in his excellency in the sky."

Such a point of reference is an exalted corrective to our human measures of excellence, necessary as they are to everyday living. What Plato pointed to in the *Republic*, when he declared, "Nothing imperfect is the measure of anything," Scripture makes very plain. In his First Corinthian Letter, St. Paul speaks of some of his contemporaries who "measure themselves by their own standards or by comparisons within their own circle, and that," he concludes, "doesn't make for accurate estimation." "No," he continues, we should rather "judge ourselves by the line of duty which God has marked out for us" (II Cor. 10:12, Phillips).

Now do not misunderstand me. There is a kind of comparison of one person with another, a considering of student achievement through marks, rating scales, and objective test results, that is essential to education. But necessary as all this is, it falls far short of the ultimate concept of excellence.

One of the Old Testament words for excellence has the two meanings of "rising" (in the sense of "loftiness") and of "pride," so reminding us that preoccupation with excellence only on the human level, apart from ultimate goals, has in it the seed of its destruction. Real competence in teaching, high standards, these qualities and others like them are expected of independent education. But there is a danger in being satisfied with these alone. As Dean Gordon of the Princeton University Chapel has said, "We like to think that knowledge saves, as will be stated in many college commencements in about two months. We are willing to gamble on the wisdom of this world. Yet," he continued, "intellectual excellence may be the means of our destruction."

Yes, there is a peril of pride to which we in independent education are susceptible. It is easy, as our standards rise, for us who are administrators and teachers to boast about the bright young people we teach. And who of us has not done this? We have our programs for the gifted, our honors courses, the newer mathematics, comprehensive language programs, and perhaps even programmed instruction, a euphemism for teaching machines. But in themselves these things are not enough. Having achieved them, should not our attitude be like that described in our Lord's parable: "We are unprofitable servants; we have done that which was our duty to do"?

Look again at our theme of excellence. I remind you that this means relating our teaching and learning to a dimension beyond that which is measured — and in its place validly so — by our human standards.

And now to the second part of our subject, which is "Our Obligation to Excellence." Let us look at this broadly and then personally. Our Christian schools and colleges are independent. This fact spells obligation in capital letters. Throughout the history of American education, and particularly in the earlier years of our country, Christian independent schools and colleges have been in the forefront of progress. But the day is past when we can claim to be superior academically to all of public education. With the development of secular and tax-supported schools and colleges, Christian education has been outstripped by secular education. And only recently have we been coming back academically into our own. But there is one great area in which the opportunity to strive for excellence is uniquely ours. And that area is the pursuit of excellence in its full spiritual and Godward direction.

None of us should minimize the earnest efforts for moral training being made in some public schools and in some secular colleges. Yet the fact remains that it is the peculiar privilege, even the birthright, of independent Christian education to teach the Bible and the Christian faith just as fully and deeply as it desires. What does this say to us? Or better, what obligation does it impose upon us? Simply this: in a time when our very survival depends upon closing the gap between technological power and moral and spiritual restraint in using that power, we in Christian education have the obligation of commitment to truth in all that we learn and teach as well as the duty to point young people to the highest examples of excellence — namely, the most excellent of all books, the Bible, and the most excellent of all persons, Jesus Christ.

I know very well that this may sound old-fashioned to some of our secular colleagues. But let us not be intimidated by what C. S. Lewis calls the chronological fallacy, by which he means dismissing ideas and values simply because they are not new. The criterion of truth is not the calendar. Whether we reach the moon and beyond, whether or not life is discovered on other planets, truth and righteousness, the difference between the knowledge of good and evil, the eternal verities, do not change. The obligation of excellence in Christian education entails, then, commitment to the truth in all that we learn and teach. Without the recognition and practice of that principle, even the most doctrinally correct education will fail to reach full excellence. So we consider for a moment or two the all-important question of our attitude to truth.

There is a human tendency to be timid about the truth. To put it plainly, there are some — and they are in both camps theologically (liberal as well as conservative) — who are afraid of the truth. They suffer from a species of *aletheiaphobia,* to coin a word from the Greek. Now when an evangelical Christian is afraid of the truth, it may be because he has equated some particular formulation with final truth. Therefore, when he sees some newly apprehended scientific truth, some breakthrough into wider knowledge as a threat to the system to which he is committed, he may react in fear and, sometimes, even in anger. But, as Plato said, "No man should be angry at what is true." And, we may add, the reason is plain; for to be angry at what is true is to be angry at God, for he is the God of truth.

On the other hand, those of more liberal persuasion theologically are prone to another kind of *aletheiaphobia.* Priding themselves upon their openness to everything new, they may see in old yet unwelcome truth a threat to their cherished ideas. Theirs is not so much the fear of the expanding aspect of truth as it is the fear of the particularity of truth. But the fact is that all truth, whether old and cherished or newly revealed, is of God. Let us welcome truth and, when we cannot understand all its implications, for this is an essential condition of our finiteness, let us be assured that there is no real inconsistency in the truth of God and that all of it is reconcilable in Christ.

What is our attitude to truth? Is it openness or timidity? Do we fear new truth or do we welcome it? Our answers to these questions reveal much about our attainment of excellence.

But hand in hand with this commitment to truth there is for Christian education that is determined to seek excellence the on-going obligation to make the Bible and him who is its chief subject the living center of its entire program.

I believe that Christian education does the young people entrusted to its care a cruel disservice if, along with the great books that are part of our heritage, it deprives them of a careful, demanding study of the greatest book. There is a poignant entry in the journal of the brilliant writer, Katherine Mansfield, who died of tuberculosis at an early age and who came upon the Bible only in her mature life, never having read or studied it until then. "I feel so bitterly," she wrote, "that I have never known these writings before. They ought to be part of my very breathing."

Let us make sure that our Christian education does not with-hold "these writings" from young people who need them per-haps more than any generation has ever needed them. If the Word of God is to be part of the very breathing of our youth, then it must be well taught to all students in the Christian school and college. Indeed, no matter how superior our work in science or the humanities is, without first-rate Bible teaching Christian education cannot really be excellent. And if Scripture is first among books, it is because its central theme is the Person who showed once and for all in human life the ulti-mate meaning of excellence. Excellence means commitment to the best to the extent of choosing it beyond the better. For me, and I believe for very many of us, the best is made known in the Person and words and, above all, in the saving work of Jesus Christ.

A leading characteristic of youth today is their search for mean-ing and identity in a confused time. Dr. MacLennan of Yale tells of a little girl in New Haven whose mother was worried because the child persisted in using wrong words in the Lord's Prayer. Her version began like this: "Our Father who art in heaven, how-do-you-know-my name?" She was not so far wrong at that. She had the unconscious insight to want to know what youth — yes, all of us — want to know, that God is near and that he knows us by name.

W. H. Auden describes it in these lines:

> *To be young means*
> *To be all on edge, to be held waiting in*
> *A packed lounge for a Personal Call*
> *From long distance, for the low voice*
> *That defines one's future....* [1]

And the Personal Call, the only call that can satisfy the heart of youth, comes from him who said of himself, "He calleth his own sheep by name."

"Our Obligation to Excellence." In its highest sense this is a personal call, a personal obligation. Goethe is said to have

------

[1] From *The Age of Anxiety*, by W. H. Auden, New York: © Random House, 1947.

remarked that the spirit tends to take to itself a body. So the idea of excellence in education must be manifest in us — not only classroom teachers but administrators also — because principals and headmasters, presidents and deans, are also teachers, teaching by their attitudes and actions. The fact is that if we are in earnest about communicating excellence, we must practice it ourselves. But this is a costly matter. The price is high and it will not come down.

Look at several aspects of that cost. More excellent teaching in the context of this discussion costs submission through faith. It entails nothing less than individual commitment to the most excellent Person, Jesus Christ, as he is set forth in the most excellent Book.

But faith must be followed by works. What are the works that we who aspire to excellence in teaching must do? Well, they are those of the mind and those of the heart. It is obligatory for us to be intellectual persons to the glory of God, and it is also necessary for us to show genuine Christian concern for our pupils. Neither is easy.

To be an intellectual person is not just to be intelligent, not just to store up credits and earn degrees; it means lifelong devotion to the things of the mind.

What of our own individual program of studies? (I address the question to all of us, faculty as well as students.) Does it contain things that are hard? All of us must have such a program. None of us is exempt from voluntary intellectual work, quite apart from graduate courses we may be doing. Before engaging a new teacher, I wish that I might look at his personal library, at the kind of books he has, and that I might find out whether they are read. Above all, I should want to know whether the Bible is a living part of his library.

Then there are the works of the heart, by which I mean the attitudes and feelings out of which we learn and teach. "And yet I show unto you a more excellent way." So St. Paul introduces the greatest of all poems on love. Here I speak especially to my teacher colleagues. More excellent teaching is teaching constrained by love — not sentimentality, but love that honors and respects and likes youth. One of our Eastern schools for boys, the Pingry School, which recently celebrated its one hundredth anniversary, has this motto, "Maxima reverentia debetur pueris." Translated freely it means "The greatest respect is due boys." Yes, and girls too, and college men and women. More excellent teaching demands imaginative concern that sees beyond youth to the mature man and woman. It costs in self-expenditure of time and effort.

More excellent teaching can be had at a price: going the hard way. For as Alfred North Whitehead said: "The art of education is never easy. To surmount its difficulties is a task worthy of the highest genius. . . . It is the training of souls." Few, if any of us, would claim genius. But we have something better. We have available to help us the greatest of teachers, if we will submit ourselves to him who is more than teacher, who is the Saviour.

Excellence — more excellent learning and teaching. To move in this direction day by day is not a beautiful ideal and nothing more. It is a live option and it faces every one of us. Not that we shall ever fully attain it. There is only One who is wholly excellent. Nevertheless we must press on in our high calling. Whether we do this and whether we are willing to pay the price of excellence is by the grace of God our own decision.

Phi Alpha Chi address at Gordon College and Divinity School, 1962.
— *Gordon Review,* 1962

Seventeen
THE AESTHETIC PROBLEM

In recent years, evangelicalism has been coming of age intellectually. With the strengthening of academic standards in many of its schools, colleges, and seminaries, its tendency toward anti-intellectualism has declined. More evangelical educational institutions have been accredited by the great regional associations since 1950 than in the preceding half-century. An increasing number of scholarly books are being written. And one of the major developments in religious publishing during the past decade has been the willingness of leading secular publishers to bring out the work of evangelical thinkers.

But a parallel tendency toward what may be called "anti-aestheticism" remains. In Dorothy Sayers's introduction to *The Man Born to Be King,* an essay every Christian student of the arts should know, she speaks of "the snobbery of the banal." It is a telling phrase, and it applies to not a few evangelicals. They are the kind of people who look down upon good music as highbrow, who confuse worship with entertainment, who deplore serious drama as worldly yet are contentedly devoted to third-rate television shows, whose tastes in reading run to the piously sentimental, and who cannot distinguish a kind of religious calendar art from honest art. For them better aesthetic standards are "egghead" and spiritually suspect.

The arts pose uncomfortable problems for many evangelicals. There are those who question the relevance of the arts to Christian life and witness in these days of world upheaval. "Why," they ask, "spend time in this tragic age talking about such things as aesthetics?" The answer is that art belongs to human life. Pervasive and influential, it is an essential element of man's environment. And when art is unworthy, man's spirit is debased. "The powerful impact of modern culture upon modern man ... discloses," as Professor W. Paul Jones of Princeton says in an important essay, "... the overwhelming degree to which contemporary man is being formed by an 'art' not really worthy of the name" ("Art as the Creator of Lived Meaning," *The Journal of Bible and Religion,* July, 1963).

Art, though aesthetically autonomous, has deep spiritual and moral implications. Like the capacity for worship, the aesthetic sense is one of the characteristics that set man apart from the animals. Evangelicals turn away from art as a side issue or frill at the peril of their own impoverishment and at the cost of ineffectiveness in their witness. For art, which is the expression of truth through beauty, cannot be brushed aside as a luxury. We who know God through his Son, who is altogether lovely, must be concerned that the art we look at, listen to, read, and use in the worship of the living God has integrity.

Our God is the God of truth. According to the Gospel of John, "He that doeth truth cometh to the light." This great principle is just as valid aesthetically as in doctrine and in practical living. Art that distorts the truth is no more pleasing to God than any other kind of untruth. Surely it is not too much to say that the God of all truth looks for integrity in artistic expression as well as in theology.

Some evangelicals may not like art. Because of their cultural illiteracy, they may be ill at ease in the presence of worthy artistic expression. In their discomfort they may want to say to the aesthetic side of life, "Go away, I'm not interested. I don't want to be bothered by you." But it will not go away. Through millions of radios and television sets, through the printed page, through advertising, through the architecture and furnishings of public buildings, churches, and homes — in a thousand and one ways art is here, though often in unworthy forms, and no one can run away from it.

Moreover, Christians have an aesthetic problem not merely because of the ubiquity of the arts but because in one way or another much in the contemporary use of literature and the arts is debased and opposed to the truth and to the values to which Christians are obligated. Evangelicals had better be concerned about the aesthetic problem, if for no other reason than that a tide of cheap and perverse artistic expression is constantly eroding the shoreline of noble standards and godly living.

The situation is complicated by the multiplication of leisure hours in this automated age. How many now use their extra hours wisely? Gresham's law may well have an aesthetic counterpart in that bad art like bad money drives out the good.

As background for some answers to the problem, consider a very brief survey of the aesthetic situation among many evangelicals today with particular reference to music, the visual arts, and literature.

Music is an area in which "the snobbery of the banal" stands in strange contrast to the doctrinal discrimination of many conservative Christians. Not only does the mediocre drive out the good; there is also a certain intolerance of the excellent that refuses to see that great music can be a far more true expression of a biblical theology than piously sentimental music. Or it may be that certain kinds of music finding ready acceptance in some churches reflect a theology that, despite its high claim to orthodoxy, yet leaves much to be desired.

Religious music, however, is not the only music we hear. Much of non-religious music — serious and not just popular in character — betrays the spiritual rootlessness and moral anarchy of the times, as in the strident and heartless works of some of the atonalists or the irrationalities of the avant-garde composers. Thus there is all the more reason for inculcating in God's people higher standards for this great art that speaks so directly to the emotions and to the spirit.

Look next at the visual arts. Here, as in music, there are great riches. Granted that much in modern painting is related to the spiritual alienation of the day (although not all abstractionism is unworthy), how slight is the acquaintance of many evangelicals with the masters, past and present. How many know the works of American masters like Stuart, Inness, Ryder, Winslow Homer, Cassatt, Marin, or Andrew Wyeth? And what of the priceless treasures of great Christian art through the ages? There is vastly more in religious painting than the ever-present head of Christ that seems almost to have become a Protestant icon.

As for literature, where are the first-rate Christian novels and poems? Evangelicals have made notable progress in scholarly writing, but their achievement in more imaginative forms of literature is mediocre. Christian editors know the paucity of verse by evangelical writers that even begins to qualify as poetry. And in the field of fiction, distinguished novels and short stories written by evangelicals today are almost nonexistent.

Perhaps one thing that holds evangelicals back is a certain cultural parochialism and fear of the world. The moral state of much contemporary literature is indeed appalling. Here the aesthetic problem is a spiritual one that cannot be divorced from the Christian conscience. But there are many books that evangelicals can and must read, including not only the great treasures of English, American, European, and other literature but also representative current writing.

At a Christian teachers' institute several years ago, I urged breadth of reading and ventured to give a brief list of some of the great works indispensable to a liberal education. In the discussion that followed, a young man asked, "What has Plato to say to a Christian?" The answer is that Plato and every other great writer and artist of the past or present has much to give a Christian not only because it is essential to know the main currents of human thought but also because genius comes only from God. The doctrine of common grace asserts that God distributes his gifts among all kinds of men — unbelievers as well as believers. But the gifts are God's and the glory is his. Amid the moral corruption of our day, some great and worthy books are being written. Christians need to know them.

Like much else, culture begins at home. Taste is formed by what we live with. The question might well be asked of evangelicals: "What does your home tell of your spiritual and intellectual and aesthetic interests?" Said Rudyard Kipling in that subtle story, entitled "They," "Men and women may sometimes, after great effort, achieve a creditable lie; but the house, which is their temple, cannot say anything save the truth of those who have lived in it."

But this brief survey, which might well be extended to other arts such as drama and architecture, while necessary as diagnosis, points clearly to the need for action. Let us consider, therefore, three proposals toward evangelical answers to the aesthetic problem: (1) the formulation of a Christian theory of aesthetics based first of all upon the insights of the Bible rather than upon extra-biblical sources; (2) the cultivation of good taste and the development of the critical faculty; (3) revision of educational programs to give a more adequate place to the arts.

(1) Consider first the study by evangelicals of the theory of aesthetics. One of the hopeful signs of the last twenty years has been the development of a Christian and biblical philosophy of education. If evangelical education is experiencing renewal, the reason is that evangelical educators have been seriously occupied in considering the theological and philosophical basis of Christian education and in defining its goals.

But so far very little study has been devoted to aesthetics. Indeed, it is difficult to bring to mind a single published book by a conservative evangelical that deals competently with the theology and philosophy of aesthetics. Only comparatively recently have any Protestants given serious thoughts to this field. Professor W. Paul Jones, in the article previously referred to, says, "Despite a history of virtual indifference to art, Protestant thinkers within the past several decades have begun to explore in earnest the relation of religion to aesthetic matters." Evangelicals should be joining in this effort. It faces them with an exciting opportunity to explore new paths in applying biblical truths to their cultural milieu.

The bulk of the work being done in the field of Christian aesthetics represents Roman and Anglo-Catholic thought. Its roots go deep into sacramental theology, Thomism, Greek philosophy, and such great writers as Dante. But in large part it is extra-biblical. There is a radical difference between the thought-forms of the Bible and those of Western philosophy and humanistic culture. And while the Bible says little directly about the arts or aesthetics, its basic insights must provide not only the foundation for an authentic Christian aesthetic but also the corrective for artistic theory derived from other sources, however excellent these may be.

Moreover, what some liberal Protestant thinkers have been doing in the field of aesthetics also needs revision, as Professor Jones clearly points out. For Paul Tillich and others like him, he says, art is important because it is chiefly the indicator or "barometer of the 'faith' or 'ultimate concern' of a generation or culture." But the difficulty, he goes on to show, is that such a view of the function of art fails to discriminate between first-rate, second-rate, third-rate art, the latter of which often reflects the present culture more truly than the first! Art belongs to the only creature made in the image of God, the only creature to whom is given in a limited but real extent the gift of creativity, even though the gift is marred in fallen human nature. Thus considered, it is much more than the faithful mirror of culture. It is far more importantly a way-shower, leading on under God to fuller visions of his truth.

If there is, as we have seen, tension between many evangelicals and the aesthetic aspect of life, the reason lies in a contented ignorance of much that is aesthetically worthy and a satisfaction with the mediocre because it is familiar. Yet theological roots in the eternal biblical verities which never change do not necessarily imply enslavement to aesthetic traditionalism.

An essential element of true aesthetic practice is, as Alfred North Whitehead has suggested, the adventure of new ideas and their development in new forms. Let us remember that the great artists of the past had in their day an element of newness and spontaneity, and the greater the art the more abiding the newness. In a time when the ugly and the formless have become a cult reflecting the confusion of the pagan world, the creative Christian spirit in art should be pointing the way forward and upward, but always with reference to the everlasting and ever-present truth of him who is "the same yesterday, and today, and forever."

(2) A second proposal is that evangelicals must, if they are really to wrestle with the aesthetic problem, take seriously their obligation to develop critical discrimination in the arts. Good models are absolutely essential for sound aesthetic judgment.

Good taste is not expensive; it is just discriminating. And it can be developed. Its formation begins very early.

It matters everything what kind of pictures are looked at by children, what kind of music is heard, what kind of television programs are viewed. Art exists in its own right, not just as a vehicle for moralism. Yet it cannot but affect those who are exposed to it. For young people to live day by day with shoddy literature and vulgar entertainment may tear down what they have heard in church and learned in Sunday school. Evangelical churches have picnics and hikes, athletic games and parties for young people — wholesome means of fellowship indeed. Why not also Christian fellowship in group attendance at a symphony concert, or a violin or piano recital? And it is surely not beyond reason for Christians to visit art galleries together. "The way to appreciate beauty," said Professor William Lyon Phelps of Yale, "is to keep looking at it, to appreciate music is to keep listening to it, to appreciate poetry is to keep reading it."

At the end of the first chapter of Romans, after his appalling catalogue of sins within the human heart and life, Paul states the ultimate condemnation of unregenerate man when he says that they "not only do the same, but have pleasure in them that do them." As people look together at what is unworthy and debased aesthetically, they are together debased. But the converse is true. The shared experience of great music or drama, living with good pictures (even in reproductions) — these are group experiences in nobility and, let it be added, in reality. Not all music is joyous, nor does all drama have a happy ending. Yet, as Aristotle shows in his *Poetics,* tragedy purges the emotions through pity and fear. And at the pinnacle of involvement through experience in the company of others is the reverent worship of the living God, not for the sake of what we get out of it, but because God is God and because worship must be given him.

The time is overdue for evangelicals to outgrow their careless unconcern for aesthetic values and to develop critical standards that will enable them to distinguish good from bad in the art that surrounds them.

111

(3) The third proposal, obvious but nonetheless important, concerns the more adequate place that the arts ought to have in Christian education. In too many evangelical schools and colleges the arts are little more than poor relatives of the curriculum. Yet in actuality they are not marginal, peripheral subjects; they are close to the heart of Christian life and witness. At present evangelical education is strongest aesthetically in music, although even here it yet has far to go. When it comes to the visual arts like painting and architecture and to the other performing arts, including drama, much of evangelical education is like a fallow field that needs both planting and cultivating. Christian schools and colleges must practice the unity of truth they preach by giving the arts a greater place in the curriculum.

The compelling motive for Christian action in the field of aesthetics lies in the nature of God. Christians are obligated to excellence because God himself is supremely excellent. In the Hall of Fame at New York University, these words are inscribed in the place given Jonathan Edwards, the greatest of American Christian philosophers: "God is the head of the universal system of existence from whom all is perfectly derived and on whom all is most absolutely dependent, whose Being and Beauty is the sum and comprehension of all existence and excellence." It is because of who and what God is, it is because of the beauty and truth manifest in his Son, it is because of the perfection of his redeeming work, that evangelicals can never be content with the mediocre in aesthetics. Here, as in all else, the call is to the unremitting pursuit of excellence to the glory of the God of all truth.

Address at Nyack Missionary College, 1964.

— *Christianity Today,* February 26, 1965

Eighteen
THE DEBASEMENT OF TASTE

To the American mind censorship is abhorrent. Unlike the totalitarian state, ours is a country in which men may speak, write, and publish as they wish and read and see what they want. Just as governmental requirements of religious and political conformity are intolerable, so censorship in literature and in the visual and performing arts is repugnant to our society. To be sure, there are legal limits to the exercise of free speech and artistic expression; the law prohibits obscenity that is utterly without social value, malicious libel, and subversion of national security amounting to "clear and present danger." Yet we seem in principle to be moving toward a position in which it will be increasingly difficult to define and enforce the limits beyond which the spoken and written word and the various modes of artistic expression may not go.

Thoughtful observers of American society can hardly fail to recognize the almost Copernican revolution that has taken place in American standards of decency. What was a trend two or three decades ago has in the last five or ten years become a landslide. The daring plays or pictures of the late fifties seem tame in comparison with today's "adult" entertainment. That a minister of a great denomination should place on the pulpit alongside the Bible a book denied free circulation since the eighteenth century because of its salaciousness ought not to be considered merely an individual aberration but should be seen for what it is — one of many signs of a changed climate of opinion that now stomachs what only a few years ago would have been spewed out as morally defiling. Of recent years the public sense of propriety has been chipped away under the ceaseless impact of literature, entertainment, and advertising that have gone further and further in unending exploitation of sex.

113

To turn to another field, the unanimous decision of the Supreme Court throwing out a $500,000 award in an Alabama libel suit against *The New York Times* has upheld the right of criticism of public officials (even though the criticism may be false) provided that it is not made "with actual malice." The decision was doubtless necessary; in a democracy political discussion must at all costs be kept free from reprisal. However, two justices, Hugo L. Black and Arthur J. Goldberg, in concurring opinions, in which Mr. Justice Douglas joined, advocated the removal of the qualification regarding malicious intent. Mr. Justice Black's call for "granting the press an absolute immunity for criticism of the way public officials do their duties" was consistent with his statement in 1962 that any and all libel and slander laws along with any prosecution whatever of spoken or written obscenity are ruled out by the First Amendment (interview with Professor Edmond Cahn, *New York University Law Review*, June, 1962). Though few would go so far as this, it is evident that the widening interpretation of the constitutional privilege of freedom of speech and the press carries with it a heavy obligation of self-restraint.

Censorship, self-restraint under liberty, or untrammeled freedom of expression in speech, the press, and the arts — which? This is the problem. There are no easy solutions. And for this reason and because no problem comes closer than this one to the springs of human conduct and welfare, it must be the subject of deeper Christian thought and concern. Certainly the present situation in which almost anything can be said, written, or portrayed may yet result in a reaction that will impose restrictions in default of the exercise by individuals and groups of socially responsible self-restraint.

Further questions need to be asked: Is the public taste descending to a point of no return through mass media that reach as never before practically all the population? The licentious Restoration drama in England led to reform through the middle class; but what if the general standard of propriety has been lowered throughout society? Or, looking at the problem from another side, is it reasonable, while assuming on the one hand that the only truly effective censorship or restraint is self-imposed, to suppose on the other hand that man in his alienation from the God of holiness and truth will exercise such self-restraint?

To such questions there are no easy answers. But they must be asked; and as they are asked, the Christian position respecting the moral relativism of the day must be clearly and unashamedly stated. It is not the task of the Church to impose its convictions upon the world, but it is the obligation of the Church to declare its convictions to the world. In a day when multitudes have substituted a laissez-faire morality for the biblical ethic, Christians are responsible to live in a non-Christian world according to the teachings of their Lord and the Scriptures which testify of him.

This leads to the responsibility to practice Christian nonconformity in a society that is brimful of materialism and sensuality, and that widely repudiates the Gospel with its ethical corollaries. And this in turn entails a Christian critique of cultural values, based not upon withdrawal or isolation from culture but upon compassionate understanding of it in the light of biblical revelation.

What, then, are some principles of Christian action in a morally corrupt society? Short of the millennium, Scripture knows no such thing as a Christian world order; with utter realism it sees the Church and the believer as in the world and therefore with responsibilities to it but at the same time as generically different from it. As a new man in Christ, the believer has in spiritual reality an other-worldly origin, although he lives in a this-worldly environment.

The inevitable result is tension. "The world," said Christ of his disciples, "has hated them because they are not of the world." What he stated with such profound simplicity is developed throughout the New Testament, especially but by no means exclusively in the Pauline epistles. But this polarity between Christians and the world does not exempt them from their continuing responsibility to be "the salt of the earth" and "the light of the world."

It is at this point of creative witness that ambiguities arise in respect to the Christian attitude toward the wide-open expression so characteristic of contemporary literature and the arts. Because these mirror the mood of the time with its restless search for meaning and escape by those who do not believe in the Gospel, many Christians feel that we must know what is being communicated. And so we must — within limits.

"But what," it may well be asked, "are these limits?" Briefly they may be comprehended under three principles: that of Christian responsibility for the thought-life, that of Christian responsibility for one's brother, and that of Christian non-conformity to the world.

Individual responsibility for the thought-life is implicit in the Sermon on the Mount, in which Christ searchingly equates sin in thought with sin in act: "Whosoever is angry with his brother without a cause shall be in danger of the judgment. . . . Whosoever looketh on a woman to lust after her hath committed adultery with her already in his heart."

To know what the world is thinking and saying does not mean willing capitulation to its obsessive preoccupation with illicit sexual activity. The argument that books like *Fanny Hill* with their descriptions of prostitution and perversion provide a useful background for choosing virtue is as sensible as advocating visiting a brothel as an inducement to chastity. No Christian is obligated to reside in the brothels of the mind in order to know the world in which he lives. For those who feel obligated to know what people are reading, sampling under Christian conscience is sufficient acquaintance with the redundant portrayal of lust that fills so many pages and occupies such unending moving-picture footage. The inescapable principle that thought leads to action has not been canceled by dropping practically all reticencies in fiction and on the screen. It is still true that as a man thinks in his heart, so he is, and that "the pure in heart shall see God."

"But what of the 'erotic' passages in the Bible?" To that question, frequently raised by defenders of morally questionable literature, the answer can only be that the attempt to equate the restrained way in which Scripture speaks of sex or the beautiful imagery of Solomon's Song with a *Tropic of Cancer* or any other scatological novel is sheer intellectual dishonesty convincing only to those who are ignorant of Scripture.

A second responsibility relates to one's brother. The glorious truth is that Christians have liberty of thought and action. They are under grace, not law. But their liberty has inherent limits. As the Apostle shows in his classic exposition of Christian liberty in Romans 14, liberty may not be exercised in such a way as to "put a stumblingblock or an occasion to fall in his brother's way." No reasonable Christian would distort this principle to the extent of subjecting all literature and art to bowdlerizing; there must be a place for honest and responsible portrayal of human life in the actuality, often unpleasant, of evil as well as good. Yet Christians cannot in the exercise of their liberty escape responsibility for youth. If promiscuity is rife among adolescents throughout the country today — including many church-going young people — the question of where they learned their "new morality" is in part answered by what paperbacks and magazines they are free to buy at the corner drugstores, what they read even in respectable periodicals, and what they see in their neighborhood theaters as well as on the television screen at home. Indifference to human welfare when responsibility for others demands restraint of personal indulgence, is a mark of our age; and it shows itself in lack of concern for what is happening to children through debasement of public taste.

A third responsibility is that of non-conformity. Christian protest is overdue. Making every allowance for contact with and understanding of the world, the call of both Church and believer is to non-conformity. Paul's "be not conformed to this world: but be ye transformed by the renewing of your mind" has ample roots in the teachings of Christ. Samuel Rutherford of seventeenth-century Scotland put the principle in vivid words, "You will find in Christianity that God aimeth in all his dealings with his children to bring them to a high contempt of, and a deadly feud with the world"— words that echo the drastic statement of James the brother of the Lord, "Know ye not that the friendship of the world is enmity with God?"

What is needed is a resurgence of Christian responsibility

117

expressed first of all in self-restraint and thoughtful discrimination of values. The wholesale avoidance of all modern literature and entertainment will not do. Not everything the world does is corrupt. Under God's common grace unbelievers write great novels and plays, paint beautiful canvases, compose fine music, and produce worthy motion pictures. Yet when the world uses its abilities to degrade public morality and debase human life, then Christians are obligated not only to non-conformity but also to open protest.

In *The Decline and Fall of the Roman Empire,* Edward Gibbon gives as one of the main causes of the growth of the early Church in the decadent empire the pure morality of the Christians, who, by their steadfast non-conformity to the world around them, shone as lights in the darkness and worked as salt in a pagan society. The principle has not changed. Purity for conscience' sake, goodness out of conviction, self-restraint motivated by love for God and man, have not lost their winsomeness. In this secular society, as in imperial Rome, Christ-like living still has its ancient power.

— *Christianity Today,* April 10, 1964

Nineteen
THE CHRISTIAN USE OF LEISURE

With the five-day work week, most Americans enjoy an amount of free time unknown to former generations. While the number of hours worked during the year fell rapidly between 1940 and 1960, the decline, although slowed since the advent of the forty-hour week, continues. But working less and less for more and more leisure is not making us a happier or a better people. Leisure time is a potential rather than an inherent good. Its beneficial employment demands the exercise of personal responsibility, for few things are so demoralizing as the abuse of leisure. What we do with our free time is a matter of Christian concern.

Underneath the misuse of leisure is the lack of those inner resources that make possible the right use of solitude. As Pascal put it in a flash of insight, "All the unhappiness of men arises from one single fact, that they cannot stay quietly in their own chamber" (*Pensées,* II, 139).

The emptiness of soul that makes solitude unbearable for so many leads to the restless search that so marks our times — the search for satisfaction through new and more exciting ways of being entertained. The shared pleasures of the group are not necessarily inferior; man is a social being, and his nature requires fellowship. But what he brings to this fellowship reflects what he is within himself. And still the paradox remains that those who are best able to entertain themselves through good reading, music, art, the personal enjoyment of nature, and other worthy avocations derive most from group recreation.

Christians today live in a state of tension with the world and its culture. Nowhere is this tension more acute than in the realm of leisure. The answer to the problem is not to list the multitudinous varieties of leisure-time pursuits, and then to declare some good and some bad. That way lies legalism. Obviously there are in the light of the Word of God things that are clearly wrong and others that are clearly right. The difficulty resides in the ambiguities about which committed Christians disagree.

Moreover, the binding obligation of witnessing for Christ cannot be discharged in a social vacuum. To ask, as did Tertullian, "What has Athens to do with Jerusalem?" and then to retreat into cultural isolationism will not do for us today. Christians must know the culture that surrounds them, if they are to make their witness understood. But there is a difference between knowledge of or about something and identification with it. Our culture contains elements the defiling nature of which we know full well and in which we participate at our soul's peril.

Here is the real point of tension respecting the Christian use of leisure. As Milton says in a great sentence in his *Areopagitica,* "I cannot praise a fugitive and cloistered virtue, unexercised and unbreathed, that never sallies out and sees her adversary, but slinks out of the race, where that immortal garland is to be run for, not without dust and heat." So the Christian in an unchristian culture must have the fortitude, as Milton says in the same context, to "see and know and yet abstain."

The Reformation doctrine of the inner witness of the Holy Spirit reaches beyond its application to the Scriptures. For those who are Christ's in a spiritually alien culture, it provides the essential safeguard in the inevitable encounter with the world in which they live and to which they are obligated to communicate the Gospel. The Spirit who indwells every Christian can be trusted to show the believer who knows his Bible where in his obligatory contacts with the culture of his time he must draw the line.

In an exhaustive study of the problem of leisure in British life *(English Life and Leisure,* by R. Seebohm Rowntree and G. R. Lavers), religion is treated along with the cinema, the stage, broadcasting, dancing, and reading, as a leisure-time pursuit. This strange misconception of the role of religion in life is all too common even among church members. Whether a Christian uses his leisure for playing a musical instrument, painting pictures, reading adventure stories, gardening, mountain climbing, bowling, or any one of a thousand other things, is an optional matter. God has given us a host of pursuits richly to enjoy. The scriptural criterion of what we may do is unequivocally stated by St. Paul in Colossians 3:17, "And whatsoever you do in word or deed, do all in the name of the Lord Jesus, giving thanks to God and the Father by him." But religion (using the word in the high sense of the practice of Christianity) is not for the believer an elective, spare-time pursuit like going to football games or bird-watching. It is life itself, and it comprehends everything Christians do and say and hear and think. To be sure, certain practices of religion, such as attendance at church, reading the Bible, visiting the sick, and helping the underprivileged, are done in time apart from the daily job. Yet the claims of Jesus Christ are all-inclusive. Nothing is ever irrelevant to him with whom we have to do.

Christ is the Lord of time — of free time as well as of working time. Those who are his are responsible for the stewardship of the time he gives them. One of the great New Testament phrases is the twice-repeated one of the Apostle, "redeeming the time" (Eph. 5:16; Col. 4:5). Our Lord himself lived under the pressing stewardship of time, as we know from his reiterated "Mine hour is not yet come."

How Christians use their time in a time-wasting world is crucial to their spiritual outreach. "Eternity — for some who can't spend one half hour profitably!" President Eliot of Harvard once exclaimed. God entrusts us with nothing more valuable than time. Without it money is valueless and the stewardship of money meaningless. Literature has few more pathetic passages than the vain plea for time at the end of Marlowe's *Faustus:*

> *Stand still, you ever-moving spheres of heaven,*
> *That time may cease, and midnight never come;*
> *Fair Nature's eye, rise, rise again, and make*
> *Perpetual day; or let this hour be but*
> *A year, a month, a week, a natural day*
> *That Faustus may repent and save his soul!*

121

The very word "leisure" implies responsibility. Central to its dictionary meaning is the idea of freedom afforded by non-working time. But in Christian life and practice freedom is *always* conditioned by responsibility. Our liberty is to be used to the glory of God. We are accountable for the stewardship of our leisure as well as of our working time. From the daily occupation there is indeed leisure, but from the unremitting exercise of Christian responsibility there is no such thing as spare time. No Christian is ever off-duty for God. Leisure and working time are equally to be accounted for to the Lord who said, "Lift up your eyes, and look on the fields; for they are white already to harvest" (John 4:35).

— *Christianity Today,* January 31, 1964

Twenty

MUSIC IN CHRISTIAN EDUCATION

What kind of music has a place in Christian life? What kind of music belongs in the school program, in the home, in the church, in the recreation of Christians? The foundation upon which our thinking about answers to these questions must rest is this: All truth is of God. Therefore, music that has integrity is part of God's truth and belongs in Christian life. Truth is not confined to the spoken and written word and to such fields as mathematics and science; it relates to the arts also.

So we consider some implications, or variations, of the theme that music is a valid part of God's all-embracing truth. Chief among them is the need for breaking down the misleading distinction between sacred and secular music.

What, after all, is sacred music? According to common practice, it is music linked either to religious words, or music written for religious use. Thus, there are Christians who, while suspicious of all so-called secular music as worldly, attend with clear conscience performances labeled sacred concerts in which a good deal of third-rate, sentimental music has been baptized, as it were, by association with Christian verse; or in which tawdry, tasteless hymn arrangements, false to any real musical integrity, are deemed religious. But is the principle of sanctification by association a valid criterion for the distinction, so common in evangelicalism, between sacred or Christian and secular or worldly music? Certainly not. Rather the only defensible criterion of the fitness of music for service as a handmaid of the glorious truths of the Gospel is its own, inherent quality, provided that it meets first of all the test of truth.

"And what," someone asks, "is truth in music?" Now it would be presumptuous to attempt anything like a comprehensive

answer to this question. But we may at least point in the
direction of an answer. Consider it negatively, first of all. Music
that is pretentious, music that is vulgar, music that reeks with
sentimentality, that shows off by resorting to empty, ear-tickling
adornment — witness the so-called evangelistic style of piano
playing — lacks integrity. As music it is not true, even though
doctrinally it may keep the best of company.

But what, positively considered, are some of the elements of
truth in music? Are they not honesty of expression, sincerity in
the sense of avoidance of the cheap and contrived? Surely they
also include such elements as simplicity and directness. But on
the other hand they do not rule out either complexity or
sophistication as opposed to artless simplicity. Bach wrote some
enormously complex music, yet there is no higher musical truth
than his. Honesty and integrity in music are not confined to the
simple and naïve.

In point of fact there is a vast body of music that has truth
and integrity, yet is not fitted for church use, although Christians may enjoy it because it is part of God's truth. For example,
the Chopin polonaises or mazurkas, beautiful as they are, do
not convey religious feeling. They have a place in the Christian's
enjoyment of music but not in church.

Is there, then, music that as music, quite apart from words or
religious association, is compatible with spiritual worship?
Surely, the answer is a clear "yes." Music is not spiritual only
by association. On the contrary, there is music that is innately
uplifting in its appeal. To be sure, it cannot by itself convey
doctrine and thus is not specifically sacred or Christian, but in
its feeling and in its effect it is spiritually elevating.

Not all of Bach's religious music was written for church use.
Some of the preludes and fugues, such as the great E-major
"Prelude and Fugue" in Book II of *The Well-Tempered
Clavichord,* are deeply spiritual. Unquestionably many of
Beethoven's slow movements, such as the wonderful *Arietta* and
variations of the last piano sonata (Op. 111), speak with a
transcendental, almost heavenly voice. To make a very personal
reference, one of my abiding memories is that of listening after
my father's funeral to the "Adagio" of Beethoven's *Violin*

Concerto. The Scriptures had indeed given me their unique comfort, yet music also spoke its lesser and wordless language of comfort. Mendelssohn's *Reformation Symphony* has its religious moments and not just because of the use of "Ein' feste Burg." But the César Franck Symphony without any such reference is also religious, even mystical, in spirit. The firm majesty of Handel, so compatible with faith, is not confined to the *Messiah.* Witness the universally familiar "Largo," which, though composed for secular use, has found such wide religious acceptance. Or take a piece like the brief Mendelssohn Song without Words, called "Consolation," which we have in some hymnals under the name "Communion"; or the Schumann "Nachtstück," which we know as the hymn tune "Canonbury." Granted that personal taste enters into comments like these, still the point is clear that there is a wealth of absolute music that in itself is conducive to worship.

My own feeling is that more of this kind of absolute music should be used in our churches, not self-consciously but unobtrusively. The question may sound radical, but is the practice of always printing on our church calendars the names and composers of preludes, postludes, and offertories a good thing? Certainly we desire to develop understanding of fine music. But a church service is not a course in music appreciation. We must be careful that in reaching out for a higher level of Christian music we do not foster what Don Hustad calls "spectatorism," in which the people look upon parts of the church musical service as a performance.

Consider an illustration from painting. A distinguished artist had finished a canvas of the Last Supper. All was done with great skill, and the chalice in particular had been portrayed most beautifully. As one after another of the artist's friends looked at the painting, they said, "What a beautiful cup!" Then the artist realized that he had diverted attention from the Lord. Taking his brush, he painted out the gorgeous chalice and substituted for it a more quietly beautiful but far less obtrusive one. So should it be with music in worship. It should not call attention to itself or monopolize the center of attraction that belongs to the Lord alone. And it may well be that the use,

125

almost anonymously, of some first-rate music that, while unfamiliar, is in itself spiritual, will help the atmosphere of worship.

"But what about gospel hymns? Must all of our church music be classical?" The questions come out of a chief point of concern in evangelical Protestant worship today. Surely the answer is that, when it comes to gospel hymns and their more formal companions, it is not a matter of "either-or" but of "both-and." For the criterion for gospel music must be the truth just as the truth is the criterion for theology. Christians ought not to tolerate a double standard in worship — namely, zeal for the truth in doctrine and disregard of the truth in art.

God's truth is wonderfully comprehensive. Some of the truest music ever written, music of greatest integrity, is folk music. Think, for example, of the nobility of some Negro spirituals. It is a mistake to confine truth in music to the classical, to the sophisticated, or to the old. Christians ought not be suspicious of music just because it is new or unfamiliar. Our respect for the classics must not obscure the fact that good music is being written in our time. And there are gospel hymns — and the number is not inconsiderable — that in sincere, artless expression are honest music. They belong in our worship and education. Included among them are hymns like "What a Friend We Have in Jesus," "Blessed Assurance," or "Saviour, Like a Shepherd Lead Us," a tune, by the way, that Dvorak wove into the last movement of his *Violincello Concerto.*

One gets a little weary of extremists who say, "Away with gospel music; it's all trash"; or of those who say, "Away with all the older hymns; they're all staid, doleful, and joyless." The antitheses are false. Not all the old, standard hymns are staid and sombre; and even the best denominational hymnals contain some hymns of negligible value that are hardly ever sung. As for classifying all gospel music as trash, this is nothing less than obscurantism. It is more difficult to be thoughtfully discriminating than to fall back upon sweeping generalization. Nevertheless, discrimination according to the truth is the only responsible answer to the tension between gospel and standard hymns.

In point of fact there is a far greater threat to the musical integrity of our evangelical worship and education than the gospel hymn. This threat is the invasion of Christian music by certain techniques of the entertainment world. With the almost universal use of TV, radio, and record players, the primary God-ordained center of education, the home, has been infiltrated by the musical devices of Hollywood and the night club. What does the habitual use of such music do in a home? The plain answer is that it debases taste and cheapens the Gospel. The writer of the editorial in the September 16, 1961, issue of *The Sunday School Times* was absolutely right in his slashing attack upon the dressing up of gospel melodies in the garments of show business. If the state of music among evangelicals leaves a great deal to be desired, then records in which the precious doctrines of our redemption are unequally yoked with the movie-theater organ or sung in the mood of cocktail-hour ballads have much for which to answer.

As a matter of fact, some forms of jazz may have more musical integrity than this kind of Christian music. As Professor Wilson Wade of Dartmouth has said, there is a type of jazz that expresses honestly the spiritual lostness and rootlessness of modern man. And while evangelicals would dissent from his conclusion that the integrity of jazz in reflecting the predicament of man today entitles it to a place in worship, there are those who would think its use as a spiritual medium to be less questionable than that of some of the shoddy music that finds acceptance among us. Paul's exhortation "Don't let the world around you squeeze you into its own mold" (Rom. 12:2, Phillips translation) is an aesthetic as well as moral imperative; and it applies as much to some of the music so popular among many Christians as it does to jazz.

Now we come to the heart of the matter, which is the formation of musical taste.

Permit me a bit of autobiography, if you will. It is my privilege to be the son of a great Bible teacher, one who stood firmly upon the Word of God and who preached the Gospel wherever he went. Why am I a Christian today? Because of God's grace in using the witness of my parents in my home, the place where, as a small boy, I received Christ as my Saviour. And why am I a musical person today? Again, because of my home. Among my earliest memories is that of hearing my father and my oldest brother playing Beethoven's *Fourth Symphony* in a four-hand piano arrangement. Or I recall waking up on one of the Sunday mornings when my father was not out preaching and hearing him play Mendelssohn. This was long before the days of radio and record players. Yet we had music in our home. My father and brother were not great pianists, but they loved and played good music. The formation of good musical taste depends on hearing fine music — not necessarily in great performance, for that was not nearly so available in my boyhood as it is now, thanks to long-playing records, but in constant hearing of great music even if in unskilled performance.

What of musical education in school and college? Here, too, the same principle holds. Whatever else we do, we must expose youth to greatness in music. Moreover, we need to tell them the difference between the good and the bad, between the worthy and the unworthy.

As headmaster of a school that stresses academic standards and college preparation in these competitive days, I deplore the imbalance of the curriculum in most of our schools. Music ought to be a major subject like English and mathematics. Yet even with the little time at our disposal some real exposure to greatness is still possible. At Stony Brook, aside from such activities as the chapel choir (which is one of our most respected extra-curricular activities), the usual class in music appreciation, private lessons on various instruments, and a rudimentary band, we try to give all our boys some personal exposure to musical greatness. Each year the whole school of two hundred plus the faculty is organized for part singing. Through weekly rehearsals we learn some great music and sing it at public occasions, such as the annual academic convocation or the baccalaureate service. Thus, we have learned choruses from the *Messiah,* a "Gloria" from one of Mozart's masses, some Bach, and this year we are working on a chorus from Haydn's *Creation*. It is refreshing to hear adolescent boys humming or singing Mozart or Handel as they walk about the campus. Again, there is regular exposure to music of truth and beauty through daily and Sunday chapel, not only in the singing of fine hymns but also through the organ. Concerts for the whole school at which distinguished artists perform fine music are a part of our program. But one speaks of these things with humility, realizing how very much should be done.

The principle remains unchanged, whatever our situation. The key to better things in Christian music is the hearing of greatness in music not only in the day or boarding school, not only in college and seminary, but in church school also. Not even the smallest child may safely be fed a diet of musical trash.

Consideration of our subject would be incomplete without a final look at ourselves. The great principle, no Christian education without Christian teachers, applies just as much to the school musician as it does to the academic teacher. No one who does not love music and know it first-hand can teach it with full effectiveness. No teacher of music in a Christian school or college, Bible institute, seminary, or church who is not himself a regenerated person, knowing through commitment of heart and life the living Lord, can teach music as an integral part of God's truth. Music is a demanding art. To achieve excellence in it requires hard discipline and unremitting work. Yet with all his devotion to it a Christian musician must keep his priorities clear. God is the source of all talent. When he gives talent, including musical talent, he gives it, not to be made an idol, but to be used to his glory. You may remember how humbly Haydn summed up his musical life. "I know," he said, "that God appointed me a task. I acknowledge it with thanks and hope and believe I have done my duty and have been useful to the world." Music is indeed a great gift; but it is the Giver, not the gift, who must have the first place in the teaching and practice of music.

In his own account of his conversion the church father, Jerome, who made the Latin translation of the Bible, tells of a

129

dream that led to his conversion. He dreamed, he says, that he appeared before the Judge. Asked who and what he was, he replied, "I am a Christian." But he who presided said: "Thou liest, thou art a follower of Cicero, not of Christ." For Jerome was a rhetorician, and his consuming interest and first love was his study of Cicero.

So the Christian musician must take care that the art to which he is devoted does not usurp the place that belongs to the Lord alone. He must be a Christian first, which means that everything without exception must be brought into captivity to the obedience of Christ, who in all things, music among them, must have the pre-eminence.

Address at the Annual Convention of the National Church Music Fellowship, Philadelphia, 1961.

— *Christianity Today,* February 2, 1962

MOUNTAIN CLIMBING

Twenty-One
MOUNTAIN VIEWS

I. MOTIVATIONS AND REWARDS

No mountaineer of any experience can long escape being asked, "Why do you climb?" It may, therefore, be just as well to begin these informal and very personal reminiscences by attempting to answer the inevitable query "Why do you climb?"

Now there may be behind that question more than idle curiosity. There may be behind it an attitude toward mountains, carried over unconsciously from the Middle Ages. Not until the end of the eighteenth century did men look at the jagged rocks and perpetual snows of the high mountains as anything but terrifying excrescences upon the face of nature. Only through first-hand knowledge, gained by exploring the glaciers and climbing the rocky heights, did fear give way to appreciation of the beauty of the great ranges. Or, if modern men have lost this fear of the mountains, they may see little use in climbing their summits. The hazards seem too great and the exercise too strenuous for most people to take the trouble to climb nowadays.

But the view of mountains reflected in the Bible is different from the superstitious awe of the Middle Ages or the unconcern of many in our times. In contrast to the general avoidance of mountains in medieval times, there are in Scripture, even more than in other ancient literature, many references to them, far outnumbering references to the other leading aspect of nature, the sea. From the mention in Genesis 8:4 of Ararat, the great 17,000-foot peak in Armenia, capped by its glittering ice dome, to Revelation 21:10, where John in his vision is transported to a high mountain, whence he sees the New Jerusalem in all her splendor, the Word of God is full of mountains. Names like Ararat, Moriah, Sinai, Horeb, Zion, Carmel, Hermon, Gerizim, and Olivet have rich associations; indeed the basic structure of

133

sacred history might be related to the mountains of Scripture. And in respect to poetry, some of the most sublime imagery in the Old Testament has to do with mountains.

But most appealing to the Christian is the place mountains occupy in the life and ministry of the Lord Jesus. To them he withdrew for solitary prayer. From a lofty summit the Devil showed him all the kingdoms of this world. Two of his greatest sermons were spoken in the hills. It may well have been on the flanks of Hermon, a great peak north of Galilee, that he was transfigured and his garments shone white as the high snows. Nor can we ever forget that the "cross on which the Prince of Glory died" was set upon a hill.

Despite this wealth of sacred association, climbing as we know it was not done in Bible times. As has already been stated, for the first seventeen hundred years of the Christian era there was little attempt to explore the great mountain ranges. Exceptions there were, of course, such as the Emperor Hadrian's climb of Etna in Sicily; the venturesome Leonardo da Vinci, who explored part of the Monte Rosa range; and the soldiers of Cortez who in 1519 struggled up the icy cone of Popocatepetl in Mexico to get sulphur. But it was the ascent of Mont Blanc by Paccard and Balmat in 1786 that began modern mountaineering. Following this conquest of the topmost point of western Europe, the British took up climbing, and in the nineteenth century first developed it as a recreation. Great Alpine summits were ascended by men like Tyndale, Leslie Stephen, Mummery, Whymper, and their Swiss, French, and Italian guides.

"But what," the nonclimber asks, "has all this to do with my question?" "Why," he persists, "*do* you climb?" The answer is that climbing mountains reflects an attitude toward them. We who find our recreation in the high hills do so because we love them. George Leigh Mallory, who with his young companion Irvine disappeared in 1924 within 1,000 feet of the summit of Mt. Everest, spoke for every mountaineer when he answered the question as to why he wanted to climb Everest by simply saying, "Because it's there."

Only the tiny minority of climbers will ever see, let alone attempt, the great Himalayan summits; yet when we look up at

Mt. Hood or Mt. Rainier, the Grand Teton or the Matterhorn, or even Mt. Washington or Mt. Katahdin, we also feel as Mallory did of Everest. Between us and the great hills there is a pull, not easy of definition, but nonetheless real. The mountain before which we stand is a challenge; our eyes measure its difficulties, and we want to know its cliffs and couloirs, snowfields, and glaciers. But the nonclimber is different. He may delight in the beauty of a mountain, but he admires it from afar.

In my own case, several mountains were the magnets that drew me to climbing. The first was Pike's Peak in the Rockies. The sight of its huge, reddish bulk looming beyond Colorado Springs stirred the urge to climb it, and a small boy's persistence (I was eleven at the time) was rewarded by the nine-mile trudge up the cog railway with my mining-engineer brother. Another mountain that helped make me a climber was Mt. Hood in the Cascades. The transcontinental train had stopped along the Columbia River, and there, piercing the blue air above the dark green forests, was the north face of Hood, a glorious pyramid clad in shining snow. For a boy of sixteen it was an unforgettable vision of mountain beauty and a challenge fulfilled by two ascents of this peak many years later. Influential also were the gentler summits of the Catskills, beloved by my father, with whom I walked many miles in those beautifully wooded and historic mountains of New York State. For he too was a lover of the hills, though not a climber in the technical sense.

Yes, we climb in response to a challenge. And the challenge has many facets. Not only is it a response to beauty; it has also in it the lure of the difficult. Modern life is a mixture of tension and luxury. While nerves are taxed by the hurry and competition of our towns and cities, physically we are becoming flabby. Very few Americans know how to walk. Where our parents would have walked — to church, to the store, round the block to visit a friend — we ride in cars. Mountaineering is a challenge, because it demands physical hardship. No one ever climbs great peaks without getting up early, usually before sunrise, without eating sparingly of simple food, without going

135

on when he is very tired, without exposure to burning sun or icy wind, and without at times overcoming fear.

These things are not easy; they spell discipline of hand and foot and emotion. But they are good in a time when the combination of nervous strain and physical softness is all too common, even among Christians. The bow that is always tightly strung loses its resiliency; and even the strongest constitution must relax. Our Lord voiced an abiding principle of the Christian life, when he said to his disciples, "Come ye yourselves apart into a desert place [quite possibly the Galilean hills], and rest a while." To be sure, mountaineering is but one of many forms of outdoor recreation, yet those of us who follow it thank God for the refreshment it brings.

Climbing, then, has its rewards, and they are not all physical. There is truth in the lines of that mystical poet, William Blake:

> *Great things are done when men and mountains meet:*
> *This is not done by jostling in the street.*

Everyone who has climbed at all extensively knows something of Blake's meaning, though he may find it hard to put into words. I think, for example, of a sunny midday in 1942 on the summit rocks of the Middle Teton in Wyoming. Preaching appointments had taken me to the Far West, and there was opportunity for some climbing. It was a memorable day from the four-o'clock start; trudging up the trail in the dark, seeing the dawn over Jackson Hole, walking in the early morning sun on the snow that filled upper Garnet Canyon early that July, climbing on crampons the frozen couloir to the col between the South and Middle Tetons, breasting the wind as it came rushing across the col from the Idaho side of the range, and finally looking for holds up the steep rocks to the summit. And the reward was just to sit there astride a sun-warmed granite block, nearly 13,000 feet above sea level, gazing down 6,000 feet on Jenny Lake, with the few buildings like toy houses, and looking up at the tremendous obelisk of the Grand Teton, soaring dramatically into the almost indigo sky. It was quiet with the utter stillness of the high solitudes. The sun shone brightly. And the stillness brought with it a deep, inner peace. Prayer and grateful rededication to the Lord who created such grandeur came almost unbidden from my heart. The long descent was made with spirit refreshed by an experience the memory of which abides as a permanent and treasured possession.

Another of the intangible rewards of climbing is the renewed sense of perspective. We go to the mountains with our problems — personal, business, or professional. And somehow, as we consider them on some friendly summit or under the heavens with the stars shining so brightly through the thin air, they do not loom large. We see them more clearly and in their proper place. At other times we may be too busy looking for the next hand- or foothold, or belaying our companion to think of them specifically, yet the mind and eye that become used to the heights and depths and spacious vistas of the mountains learn to evaluate the daily problems from the perspective of truth rather than the distortion of worry.

William Blake is right: "Great things *are* done when men and mountains meet." The climber may find it hard to put all these things into words for others to understand. But he knows that the intangible compensations of climbing can never be gained by "jostling in the street." They come through strenuous exertion, through the discipline of mastery over self, and, in their highest expression, through renewal of the faith that sees in the God of creation one so great that he "weighed the mountains in scales, and the hills in a balance," yet so gracious that he gave his Son, through whom all things were made, for the redemption of us men.

II. ANALOGY OF LIFE

Climbing a high mountain is much like life itself — a varied experience, sometimes pleasurable, sometimes painful, and often neither extremely pleasurable nor very painful, but just steady plodding. Either stress of danger or awareness of beauty may so intensify perception that a wealth of experience is crowded into a moment. At other times, as when the climber trudges toward a summit that appears never to come nearer, moments seem like hours. And in the higher ascents there is more plodding than excitement. The inspired moments and the achieve-

137

ment of standing on a coveted summit come, but they must be earned. On the title page of his autobiography, Dr. Abraham Flexner, whose work revolutionized medical education in America, has this quotation from the Greek poet Hesiod: "Before the gates of excellence the high gods have placed sweat." So with the mountains; the cost of gaining the lofty peaks is exertion and plenty of it.

There comes to mind an ascent of the Mount of the Holy Cross in Colorado. This peak, just over 14,000 feet and bearing on the red rocks of its face a gigantic cross made by two snow-filled gullies, is nationally famous. However, it is known chiefly by name and picture. Few tourists ever see it because it is off the beaten path; few climb it because it is so troublesome to reach. It was in the company of Joseph T. Radel, at that time Assistant Supervisor of the San Isabel National Forest, that I ascended this noble mountain in July, 1948.

Making a predawn start from a camp outside Leadville, we drove to a point near the little town of Minturn, above which the trail began and led up to a pass at an elevation of about 11,000 feet. Here it dropped with disconcerting steepness about a thousand feet into a wooded canyon, through which a stream rushed.

We stopped briefly at an abandoned cabin by the side of the stream and, crossing over, made our way upward. It had begun to rain. The vague trail mounted through timber to the tree line, where in the rocks it dwindled away. Clouds shrouded the mountain, but we kept on over jumbled boulders, gaining a ridge which disappeared into the mist. At intervals along this ridge were a few stones placed on top of each other; these we followed. The ridge was composed of a number of small humps and, as each loomed through the clouds and was topped, there was still another ahead. Momentarily the mist thinned, showing through the drizzle the true summit, distorted in the half-light and towering over us in discouraging bulk. But we kept on until, after a scramble up the summit rocks, we found ourselves at last on the peak. There was no view — only the cold, swirling mist. The register in the cairn recorded climbs several years before by an officer in the mountain troops and a professor of engineering.

It was too cold and wet to linger at the summit, so we clambered down the ridge, guided again by the little stone piles. Zigzagging the mountainside at timber line put us on the trail, and late in the afternoon we were once more at the cabin in the canyon. Now very tired, we rested before setting our jaws for the interminable climb up and out of the canyon. It is a wearisome business to toil upward when coming back from a climb, yet sometimes it has to be done. All things have their end, however, and in the dark the pass was reached and the trail followed to the car.

The weather had been dreary, the climb mostly drudgery, spacious views well nigh nil. But the day remains indelibly and not at all unpleasantly impressed in memory. The summit was one I had long wanted to climb. We saw the mountains in one of their less friendly moods. And yet the dark day had a somber beauty. Best of all was a sense of accomplishment in doing something hard.

Life's journey is for the Christian an ascent, though not one of unbroken progress. There are valleys to be descended and climbed out of. There are humiliations and defeats to be endured. The way is not always pleasant. Like the summit ridge of the Mount of the Holy Cross on that day in 1948, the path is often obscured by mist and hidden in clouds. But as we go on, we realize that we are not alone. When my friend and I saw the little rock piles on the ridge — just two or three stones, resting on each other — we knew that someone had been there before. Often we could see just one marker at a time, but were sure that another lay beyond. So with life. The whole way is not plain. Many times it takes us through black clouds. Yet Someone has gone before. And with confident faith we follow "in his steps," knowing that Christ is leading on.

After all, mountains are climbed just by putting one foot above another over and over again until the summit is reached. True, there are specialized techniques — rock-climbing, snow-craft, ice-work — yet basic to them all is the simple matter of lifting one foot after the other. You get tired, and cold, and wet, but you go on. And when you have gone on long enough you are at last there — on top. That is how Everest was climbed. Despite all the planning and strategy and equipment of that great expedition, it would have come to nought, had not Hillary and Tenzing Norkey, and the others in Col. Hunt's brave band gone on when dead tiredness and altitude made even a single upward step a tremendous effort. They just kept putting one foot above another until they stood on the earth's topmost pinnacle.

The analogy holds for all true achievement. In his old age, William Carey, the erstwhile shoemaker who opened India for foreign missions and by self-education became a master linguist for the glory of God, said to his nephew: "Eustace, if after my removal anyone should think it worth his while to write my life, I will give you a criterion. . . . If he gives me credit for being a plodder, he will describe me justly. Anything beyond this will be too much. I can plod."

There can indeed be no great achievement without plodding. Yet by itself even plodding is not enough. A climb in the Selkirks of British Columbia during the summer of 1951 made that painfully clear. The objective was Mt. Sir Donald, the dominant peak in that part of the range. It was to be a long climb, for we planned to traverse the mountain, ascending the great northwest arête and descending via the glacier. Ordinarily this climb is made from a bivouac not far from the beginning of the arête, but the guide with whom I was climbing felt that by making a very early start we could do the traverse in one day, even though a vertical ascent of nearly 7,000 feet, some of it rock-work comparable to the Matterhorn, was required.

Mt. Sir Donald is a peak of a different order from the Colorado Rockies. There is a spectacular view of it from the Canadian Pacific Railway at Glacier, B.C. Few who see the vast triangle of gray rock, piercing the sky at an appalling angle, ever forget the sight. It is a formidable climb, though not of extreme difficulty for the experienced.

It was about 3:30 a.m., and dark, as we left the Wheeler Hut of the Canadian Alpine Club. The first several thousand feet were by trail. Neither of us had climbed the mountain before, but the route had been explained the previous evening. In the cool dawn air we walked cheerfully upward, watching the early sunlight slant through the evergreens into the valley. A while after dawn, the guide said, "We're too far north; I think the mountain is back there." Brief discussion convinced us that the trail must somehow double back on itself, so on we went, steadily mounting higher. Nearing the end of the timber, we stopped and looked in consternation. Between us and our peak were two other summits, Mts. Eagle and Uto! We were miles from Sir Donald, and it was after six o'clock. (What had happened was that we had taken a wrong turn within minutes of our start. Busily talking, we had completely missed the way in the predawn darkness.)

There were two alternatives — to go back and give up the climb, or to angle through the high timber round the base of Mt. Eagle and then to go up the steep slopes into the cirque between Eagle, Uto, and Sir Donald, thus reaching the base of the arête. The latter was our choice; anyone familiar with British Columbia timber will appreciate the price we paid for our error. Strenuous effort brought us above timber line and into the cirque. Now the real ascent began, as we mounted the cliff to the foot of the arête. Here we roped for the climb of the superb ridge, sometimes so thin that one sat astride the rocks, and so steep that it soars overhead like a great staircase made for gargantuan legs. A party of young men from the Harvard Mountaineering Club was also on the mountain; since in roped climbing two make much better time than a larger group, we soon passed them. The sun warmed the rocks; the sky was a clear azure. Except for the fatigue of our long detour, it was a thoroughly enjoyable though somewhat fast climb, for we did the arête in about four and one-half hours. From the sharp little summit there was a drop of about 8,000 feet to the east into the deep trench of the Beaver River. Far below to the southwest was the high névé of the Illecilleweat Glacier, and ranged in the distance was the magnificent profusion of snowy Selkirk peaks.

Time on the summit was limited; it was nearing two o'clock and a long descent was ahead. The route down Mt. Sir Donald is complicated, but the guide sensed the way as we dropped carefully from ledge to ledge. At length we came to an over-hanging chimney of some difficulty. Belayed from above, I managed to get down it. The guide followed. It was a lesson in rock technique to see him back down this vertical crack, climbing over and outside the overhangs. I waited anxiously below, knowing that a fall in such a place might be disastrous. All went well until the last overhang. With the help of the rope I had come over it, but the guide had no such aid. He stopped climbing and called down. Quickly I climbed to a ledge below him, getting high enough for his feet just to scrape my shoulder; then, stepping on my shoulder, he eased himself down.

From this point the descent to the final cliffs above the Vaux Glacier was rapid. The next problem — to find a way across the bergschrund — was soon solved by a snowbridge. The glacier was easy, a bath in the icy glacier stream in the hot evening sun refreshing. After some bushwhacking through the heavy growth of alders, we struck the upper part of the trail to the valley. It was dark when we arrived at the hut, thoroughly weary from seventeen hours of climbing.

At dawn we had taken a wrong turning. We had plodded on, thinking we were on the right path, yet with every step moving farther from our goal. Then a vantage point gave us our bearings. Once the error was realized, the wrong way had to be given up and an entirely new direction taken.

There are many people in a similar case spiritually. They are hopefully and sincerely going on in the wrong way. They need above all to stop and look, realizing that sincerity in error can never bring them to God. Conversion is nothing less than a radical change in life's direction, and heaven is reached only through the right-about-face of complete commitment to the Redeemer. The one way to God is through him who said, "I am the way, the truth, and the life: no man cometh unto the Father, but by me."

III. SOME LESSONS

Mountaineering has sometimes been defined as the art of ascending mountains with a maximum of enjoyment and a minimum of danger. All high mountains have their perils, while the Himalayan, Andean, or Alaskan peaks present peculiar hazards of weather, avalanche, and altitude. The few who attempt Everest or K2, McKinley or Aconcagua, know their dangers. Most of us, however, are content to climb ranges like the Rockies and the Alps, which, though lacking the immensity of the Himalayas, remain in their own right great mountains.

As a matter of fact, any sizable mountain must be taken seriously. Whoever fails to do so, climbs at undue risk. By Alpine or Sierra standards, New Hampshire's Mt. Washington is not a big peak. Yet its long list of fatalities is made up in good part of climbers who underestimated its savage weather. The Cumberland hills of England barely top 3,000 feet, but their cliffs and high fells have taken severe toll of the unwary.

Among our great American mountains is Shasta in northern California. An isolated volcano, rising from a base only a few thousand feet above sea level, it towers to a height of 14,161 feet. Its massive snow-clad cone with the subsidiary crater of Shastina dominates the evergreen forests around it.

A trip to the West Coast for some conference engagements afforded an opportunity to ascend this majestic peak. Breaking the train journey from San Francisco to Portland, I stopped over at the little town of Mt. Shasta, which looks up from the west to the white summit. A truck took me to the end of the deeply rutted road on Shasta's flanks, and early afternoon found me, ice ax in hand and rucksack on shoulders, en route to the stone cabin of the Sierra Club at timber line. There I was to meet the University of Illinois geology student who was spending the summer as cabin caretaker. Because my train left the following evening, the ascent had to be made the next day or not at all.

To get up at 2 a.m. was not easy, but the thought of standing on Shasta's top was an effective alarm. My companion, a blond young giant, was practically without climbing experience, having made an unsuccessful attempt on the mountain earlier in the summer. His equipment consisted of a small tree stripped of bark, in lieu of an alpenstock, and homemade crampons, consisting of pieces of heavy tin through which were driven sharpened bolts to help footing on the icy snow.

143

It was bitter cold in the small hours of the morning, as the wind swept the frozen slopes. We toiled upward, watching the dawn gradually dispel the shadows on this west side of the peak. Then, with blinding radiance, the sun struck the snow. Quickly we donned dark glasses and covered faces and hands with protective lotion.

Visible on the skyline was a rocky point called, from its shape, the Thumb. Toward it we trudged. In climbing of this kind a line from Bishop Heber's hymn, "The Son of God Goes Forth to War," sometimes runs through my thoughts — "They climbed the steep ascent of heaven/Through peril, toil, and pain"— though in this instance, there was actually little peril. The rocks reached, we paused to eat an orange before tackling the several thousand feet of upward sloping snows that cover the ancient crater. The true summit is atop some yellow volcanic rocks, disintegrating and loose, which on this July day were fantastically decorated with frost feathers. Drawing near the rocks, we could smell the sulphur fumes issuing from the crater floor and see spots where the heat of the slumbering volcanic fires had melted the snow.

The summit commanded views to all points of the compass and as far as eye could see. Few are the mountains from which it is possible to look down 11,000 feet over a sea of green forests and billowing ranges. On the southeastern horizon rose the cone of Mt. Lassen, America's only active volcano; to the north the mountains of Oregon — McLoughlin, Thielsen, the Three Sisters — thrust skyward. And halfway between us and the forests at our feet flew a plane so small to the sight that it looked like a bumblebee.

Descending to the Thumb was a matter of trotting downhill in loose-jointed but alert relaxation. Whereupon, taking from our rucksacks pieces of oilcloth, we sat on them and in a matter of moments slid down the steep snow that had taken weary hours to climb. Reaching more level ground, my companion hastened ahead, while I sauntered after him. All at once I was sprawled out, one leg hip deep in the snow!

Now there are some things every climber should know, and among them is the fact that snow surrounding large stones is invariably treacherous. This is because the sun heats the rocks to comparatively high temperatures and the heated rock melts the snow next the boulder. Thus any step in snow close to a big rock should either be completely avoided or else carefully tested. Obviously the sudden plunge of a leg through softened snow can all too readily snap a bone. This time, and providentially, no harm was done. Shasta had simply reminded me that no climber can ever be off guard. A climb is not over until the bottom is reached. In fact, most accidents in the mountains occur on the descent and then in the easier places. It is when the climber is tired out and walking carelessly along, pleased perhaps with his ascent, that the sudden slip or incautious step brings accident.

"Pride," says Solomon, "goeth before destruction, and an haughty spirit before a fall." Times of success and unusual blessing in Christian living may be followed by moral and spiritual failure, unless accepted in humble dependence upon the Lord. Many a child of God has fallen into sin because he has never learned how to come down from a mountaintop experience. As Emile Cailliet puts it, "The greater our victories in the spiritual realm, the more painful the trials that are sure to follow in quick succession."

But not all mishaps happen in easy places or while descending. Picture a party of four men roped together on the ledges of a rarely climbed peak in Canada's Jasper National Park. They are attempting the third ascent of Mt. Oubliette (10,100 feet), part of the great wall that, with hanging glacier on its gray face, soars about 4,000 feet straight up from the colorful Amethyst Lakes. They have climbed up steep Para Pass, cutting with ice ax through the snow cornice at its top, and, hastening on, have traversed Mt. Paragon, adjoining the pass, on a small horizontal ledge, covered with loose stones. Crossing the col between Paragon and Oubliette, they have been working their way up from ledge to ledge on the face of Oubliette. The position is exposed, the outlook grand, with precipitous Mt. Geikie in the near distance, while far off on the lavender horizon looms the tremendous bulk of Mt. Robson, monarch of the Canadian Rockies.

The leader, an accomplished rock climber, is inching his way up a sheer wall; the second man waits on a ledge a few feet below him; a little lower the third and fourth man stand on a broader ledge. Suddenly and wordlessly the leader falls; passing the second and third men, he twists in midair and, still clutching his ice ax, lands on the shoulders of the fourth man, who collapses with him on the ledge but does not roll over. For a moment all is quiet. Then the other two move forward to help their companions. The leader is unhurt, his friend on whom he has fallen only dazed. Little is said, but each is thinking what might have been had the two gone over the ledge. The rope might have held; the fall might have been checked. Yet the strain of two falling bodies is very great. One thinks soberly at such a time; I know, for I was the third man on the rope. Thankfully we pulled ourselves together and went on to complete the climb.

In his *Scrambles Amongst the Alps,* one of the classics of mountain literature, Edward Whymper prefaces a chapter with the words of Euripides, "How pleasant it is for him who is saved to remember his danger." There is real insight in those words; human nature takes a certain delight in narrow escapes, and some escapes become narrower with the passage of time. But the foregoing experience has not been related with a desire just to take pleasure in the remembrance of danger. Rather do I look back upon it as a wonderful example of God's gracious protection. Without question we were saved that day from what might have been a terrible accident.

IV. THE SPACIOUS PALACES OF MEMORY

Not the least among the compensations of climbing is a memory stored with pictures that those remaining in the valleys never see. Surely one of the results of an active love for mountains is the enrichment of what Augustine in his *Confessions* called "the fields and spacious palaces" of memory. To the lover of the high places of God's creation, there is continuing joy in the remembrance of beauty experienced in personal encounter with the hills. A mountain climbed, especially if the ascent has taxed strength and skill, is a mountain that has become personalized for the climber. Memories of its individuality and structure, recollections of storm and sunshine, views awesome and friendly, heartwarming remembrance of goodly fellowship in tent, at the campfire, and on the rope — these become part of the mental furnishing of those who find recreation in the mountains. Whoever comes to climbing with receptive heart and seeing eye will find much that, being true and pure, lovely and of good report, belongs in the charter of Christian thought set forth in the last chapter of Philippians.

Let me share a few vignettes from my gallery of remembrance. The locale of the first is Mt. Orizaba, the great volcano on the border of the states of Puebla and Vera Cruz, rising to 18,696 feet — the loftiest summit in Mexico. Called by the Aztecs "Citlaltepetl," meaning "Star Mountain," it reflects the first glint of dawn and holds the rosy alpenglow when all else is dark. To stand on its graceful summit more than three and one-half miles above sea level, the third highest point in North America, brought deep satisfaction. But the picture now before me is of the bivouac before the ascent. As my friend Alfred Jackson and I sat before the campfire at timber line, we pointed to the star-decked sky and said to the native Indian guides, whose English was, if anything, less than our fragmentary Spanish, "God is great." Instantly there was a response, as the Indians uncovered their heads and looked devoutly up. We spoke of the *divino Salvador,* and tried to indicate our faith in him and his Word. A while later I lay in my sleeping bag, looking up through the thin, cold air at stars that seemed as close as incandescent lights in a vaulted ceiling. At 14,000 feet, sleep was difficult, but the splendor overhead made insomnia a triviality. Just to lie there, gazing at the magnificence of the firmament, gave blessed clarity of thought, as I meditated upon God's infinite goodness throughout the years and prayed.

Quite different is the memory of the upper part of the East Ridge of the Grand Teton in Wyoming. This ridge is one of the great American ascents — a long climb, alternating between difficult rock and precipitous snow. We were on steep slabs below the final snowfield, when we heard thunder. Black clouds sped past. Exposed rocks at about 13,000 feet are no place to be in an electric storm, but the East Ridge of the Grand Teton is not to be descended with impunity. The only retreat was to advance. We kept on. The storm, though bringing some hail, did not come near enough to launch lightning at us, and soon swept past.

Sometimes God puts us in places of severe testing. We want to turn back, but, as we plan retreat, we see no way down to the valley of placid living. The only way is up. And, lo, as the storm is weathered, God brings us out into the sunlight of his favor.

From Wyoming, to the French Alps is nearly six thousand miles, yet memory knows no distance. So the scene in my hall of recollection changes to the Grand Charmoz, one of the aiguilles that point to the dome of Mont Blanc like the spires surrounding a great cathedral. Arriving in Chamonix late one September, I made what was probably the last ascent of the Charmoz before the snows set in that year. My guide was Lionel Terray, one of the French expedition whose conquest of Annapurna presaged the fall of Everest and Nanga Parbat. Plodding knee-deep in snow up the Nantillons Glacier was hard work. At the base of the great rock wall, we put on the rope. Moving together when difficulties were less pronounced, and singly when pitches were hard, we mounted to the famous Burgener Chimney, badly iced and very severe this late in the season.

Then came the glorious summit ridge, a series of thin spires over which the climber moves with balanced care on tiny but solid holds. Thousands of feet below is the broad ribbon of the Mer de Glace; on the other side is the white cascade of the Nantillons Glacier. So sheer are the pinnacles that the climber comes down the last one *en rappel*. This kind of climbing is absorbing. Everything is forgotten except the next hand- or foothold and the glorious outlook when one pauses to rest. For all but the most expert amateur, such climbs are to be attempted only with a professional guide. Once the guide is chosen, there must be complete committal to his skill and judgment.

Among the charms of climbing is variety. Thus memory turns from France to our Pacific Northwest. I see a small fire on one of the high moraines of Mt. St. Helens, a queenly peak as perfect as Fujiyama. It is early morning and very cold. My fellow climber has lit some small sticks of pressed fiber, carried in his pack for such a time as this. We take off our gloves and warm our numbed hands while dawn streaks the sky.

There sits a grasshopper, sharing the warmth of the little fire. The tiny creature, which crept unafraid from the glacial debris to enjoy the little blaze, warms my heart with a feeling of the marvel of the life God has conferred on humble insects as well as on those who bear his image. We watch our small companion quietly; to molest him would be a profanation. It is thirteen years since that stray grasshopper joined our fireside, yet the picture of his tiny equine face watching the flame has not faded.

Lest reminiscence become wearisome, these recollections must end. Let our final thought be that of companionship. It is possible to climb alone, though those who do it multiply dangers; a sprained ankle or broken leg in a remote place may spell disaster if one is by himself. It is possible also to go through life alone, though no man by his own effort ever reaches heaven. Our humanity has its lonely aspect; each of us has thoughts and feelings not quite the same as any other human being; our hearts crave understanding. God has answered that craving. Among all the Scripture names of Christ, none is more precious to the believing heart than the single word, "Immanuel" — "God with us." No Christian is an "island," for no Christian walks through life alone.

Not every mountain ascent is completed; the records of all experienced climbers contain "misses," when, for safety's sake, the leader has wisely stopped short of the summit. Neither does every endeavor in Christian living come to a successful conclusion; sometimes our divine Leader has to take us on a detour. But when it comes to the final goal, ultimate arrival before him in whose presence is fullness of joy forevermore is assured.

— *The Sunday School Times,* August 8, 15, 22, 29, 1953

Twenty-Two
AN UNREALIZED HAZARD

In the little town of Moose, Wyoming, there is a log chapel. A small building, it is known far and wide, because behind the altar there is a spacious window through which the worshipper may see one of the grandest of mountain views — the jagged Teton peaks thrusting their snow-streaked spires heavenward. The church is named "The Chapel of the Transfiguration," after that strange and mysterious scene so vividly described in the New Testament, when Jesus went with Peter, James, and John to a high mountain — perhaps 9000-foot Mt. Hermon north of Galilee — where, while he was praying, his divine glory broke through his humanity, his face shone with the brilliance of the sun, and his garments gleamed with the dazzling whiteness of Alpine snows. And then, after a cloud came and overshadowed them, a voice spoke from the cloud, saying, "This is my beloved Son; hear him."

Let this scene be a guide to our thinking about some of the intangible aspects of mountaineering. In regard to their religious background, a group of mountaineers generally presents a broad diversity. Yet Jesus Christ is not a denominational figure, but the Saviour of the whole world. Therefore, he is not the possession of any one church, and his truth is for all of us.

Every climber knows how fully a holiday in the hills brings refreshment from daily cares. The sense of physical renewal after days of hard climbing belongs only to those willing to pay a price in self-discipline. Nor are the rewards just physical; the perseverance gained through going on putting one foot after another when dead tired, the consideration learned through group effort, the subtle but powerful influences of mountain grandeur, even a quiet kind of courage — these are some of the deeper rewards.

There is, however, another aspect of mountaineering that calls for recognition. And that is its danger. The responsible climber knows the major natural perils, such as loose rock, unstable snow, thinly covered crevasses, electrical storms. But by no means every responsible climber knows that the mountains also have their unrealized hazards. Ours is a fascinating recreation, laying compelling hold upon its adherents. A leading token of its power is the distinguished writing that it has stimulated. Other sports have their dedicated followers; few, if any of them, have produced a literature comparable to that of mountaineering. Yet in the very devotion that high mountains inspire there lies a hidden peril.

One November day several of us were scrambling up the fractured boulders piled over the summit of Mount Princeton in the Sawatch Range of Colorado. On a nearby ridge, slightly above us, was a sturdy figure, clad in windbreaker and shorts, ice ax in hand, climbing strongly to the top. We met on the summit, and, as we talked, spoke of climbing and what it meant to us. Our new acquaintance had driven many hundreds of miles through the night to climb this peak and several other fourteen-thousanders. And in answer to a remark about his obvious love of the mountains, he quietly said: "Mountains are my religion."

Now it would hardly be possible to put the chief spiritual hazard of climbing in fewer words than those. You see, such an affirmation or credo, which is by no means unique, betrays a confusion of values. For one thing, it rests upon a common but erroneous reading of the opening words of the One Hundred Twenty-first Psalm, in which the hills, rather than the Lord who made them, are seen as the source of our help. Quite otherwise is the true meaning of these oft-quoted words, as the beautiful paraphrase by the Duke of Argyll so clearly shows:

> *Unto the hills around do I lift up*
> *My longing eyes:*
> *O whence for me shall my salvation come,*
> *From whence arise?*
> *From God the Lord doth come my certain aid,*
> *From God the Lord, who heaven and earth hath made.*

151

Writing in *The Alpine Journal* on "Alpine Mysticism and Cold Philosophy," Sir Arnold Lunn says: "Mountaineering is neither a civic duty nor a substitute for religion. It is a sport, for we climb not to benefit the human race, but to amuse ourselves. . . ." And then he makes a wise observation: "All evil, as a great medieval thinker remarked, is the mistaking of means for ends. Mountaineering is not an end to itself, but a means to an end."

What, then, is the answer to this misconception in which the means are mistaken for the end and recreation substituted for religion? The answer comes from the mountains themselves, as they speak by implication to all who have eyes to see and ears to hear. Those who can discern behind the geology of the great hills the Lord who made them cannot but learn the lesson of the reverential awe, the authentic fear of the Lord, that is the beginning of wisdom. This is a lesson the world needs to learn all over again. For behind the problems of our times is the fact that men, having given up the fear of the Lord which humbles and ennobles us, have substituted for it the fear of man which enslaves our spirit.

But the voice spoke from the cloud on Mount Hermon and said: "This is my beloved Son; hear him." The New Testament does not hesitate to make the tremendous spiritual equation of identifying the Son of God with the Creator of all things. In one of the most spacious sentences ever written, St. Paul puts it this way: "By him [Christ] were all things created, that are in heaven, and that are in earth, visible and invisible, whether they be thrones, or dominions, or principalities or powers: all things were created by him and for him: and he is before all things, and by him all things consist." The spiritually sensitive climber in the Alps can hardly help being moved when he sees the cross on the summit of the Matterhorn and when he passes the wayside shrines on the trails to the high huts. For there is no incongruity in meeting these reminders of the Son of God in the high mountains. The Lord and the mountains belong together.

Mountains are great; we are small. Every climber has been reminded of this as he has seen another party on a glacier below him or on a ridge above him, looking like tiny specks in the vast landscape of snow, ice, and rock. And God is great, and we are small. In a higher realm than the physical, God is great in his infinite power and wisdom, in his enduring love and unchanging holiness. But we are small and finite, imperfect and unholy. Thus our littleness in comparison with the bigness of the mountains speaks of our need of help through him who is the Rock of Ages.

On a May day in 1953 two men, Tenzing Norkey and Edmund Hillary, stood on the apex of the earth's surface. On the same day, men were doubtless at work in the deepest mine in South India. The differential between the deepest mine and the highest mountain is great. But whether on Everest's summit or in the deepest mine, men miss the stars. So it is with humanity in general. Despite differences in character and morality, all of us have missed the heavenly standard. As St. Paul says in a great universal statement to which none of us is an exception: "All have sinned and come short of the glory of God." Therefore, we need the Lord to whom the mountains point to do for us what we cannot do for ourselves and fit us for the glory of God.

In the Epistle to the Hebrews, there is a sentence that mountaineers can appreciate. J. B. Phillips, in his *Letters to Young Churches,* translates it like this: "It was right and proper that, in bringing many sons to glory, God . . . should make the leader of their salvation a perfect leader through suffering." There are many climbers skillful enough to ascend high mountains leaderless or guideless. But no man can reach God through guideless climbing in the journey of life.

One of the distinguished contributions to mountaineering in recent years is the Sierra Club booklet, *Belaying the Leader,* with its precise tabulation of rope stresses and its classic exposition of the dynamic belay. Its beginning is impressive: " 'A leader,' wrote Geoffrey Winthrop Young, 'absolutely must not fall.' "

But the leader does fall; occasionally he does slip. We need constantly to be reminded that all human leadership — and this includes climbing leadership — is liable to err, as those of us who have seen a leader fall will never forget. But there is for this troubled age, beset with problems of a complexity undreamed of by other generations, a Leader who can never fall. Because he is the Perfect Leader, made so through suffering on the cross that he might bring us to God, we may reverently say, he needs no belay. And it is of this divine Leader that the mountains speak; through their greatness, they remind us of "the Lord who heaven and earth hath made." Silently but eloquently they are saying, "Hear him." And really to heed their message will keep us who know and love the mountains from mistaking means for ends and substituting even the finest recreation for faith in the living God.

Based on a sermon given at the annual Sunday service at the Goodsirs Camp of The Alpine Club of Canada in the Ottertail Range of British Columbia, 1 August 1954.

— *American Alpine Journal,* 1958

THE CHURCH'S TASK
AND MESSAGE

Twenty-Three

IS THE CHURCH FINISHED?

Since its beginning, the Christian Church has been attacked by its enemies. Church history is a record not of peace but of conflict. In the very words with which he established the Church, Christ pointed to this state of conflict when he said, "The gates of hell shall not prevail against it."

The attack upon the Church has come from two sides — from without and from within. In the long history of Christianity, assaults upon the Church of Jesus Christ have assumed protean forms. From apostolic times, the Church has had its heretics and apostates, its antinomians and hypocrites, who have marred its testimony. And its conflict with the world has been unremitting.

Seldom, however, has the attack from within the Church taken the form it has assumed within Protestantism in recent years. The tendency, now acute, to throw up the sponge and declare the Church itself passé and irrelevant is something new. It is a peculiarly Protestant manifestation; the very structure and nature of Roman Catholicism rule it out from that communion. So we have the ironic spectacle of Rome on the march toward renewal while within Protestantism influential voices say that this is for the Church a post-Christian era. The Church, they tell us, has lost out and is no longer relevant to the needs of men.

The mood of secular man today is one of alienation. Since he no longer believes that the world was created by a benevolent Father, the universe has become for him an unfriendly place. Its hostility threatens his existence. In a counter-defensive measure, he is driven to subject his very existence to philosophical examination. The resultant philosophical existentialism, combined with a psychology that probes man's inner spirit, has produced

157

an age of acute introspection. An alien in an alien universe must now search desperately for his identity. This secular man — this alien who has been mysteriously thrust into being in a universe hostile to his existence and bent on his destruction — must discover who he is. Alienated from the universe, secular man has become a stranger to himself. What was once a wholesome philosophical investigation of the world and a wholesome psychological exercise in self-examination has become in our time a morbid preoccupation with the self.

And now this introspective preoccupation has been projected into the Church, so that the institution founded by Christ and commissioned by him to proclaim his saving message has itself, in the minds of some, become lost. Thus we have the paradox of a Church that, according to certain influential spokesmen, does not know what it is and what it is to do, presuming to speak to men and women who do not know who they are.

It is time such assumptions about the Church and its irrelevance were challenged from within the Church. The Church has its faults. As with the individuals of which it is composed, it stands under the judgment of the living God. But with all its faults, the Church is the Body of Jesus Christ. It is more than an organization. As has been well said, it is not man-made but God-born. Today it needs renewal. It needs to be recalled to its primary function of proclaiming the Gospel of its divine Lord. It needs in his name to minister more compassionately, more lovingly, and more sacrificially to the needs of this lost world. It needs to speak to men and women where they are and in language they can understand. It needs to speak in the eloquence of deed as well as word. But in all its effort to be understood, it must never trim or accommodate the Gospel committed to it by its great Head.

Who is most vociferous in the claim that the Church is outmoded and irrelevant? Who speaks of the Church in existential terms of alienation? The answer is a liberal minority that has long since repudiated the authority of the Bible and the basic doctrines of Christianity. The vital evangelical center of the Church does not talk this way. Missionaries faced with the hard resistance of Islam, the animistic superstitions of primitive peoples, or the myriad deities of Hinduism do not indulge in defeatism. They are too busy for this kind of existential morbidity. So also with evangelicals at home, whether in pulpits and parish, in Christian education, or in home and rescue mission work.

The answer to the readiness of some to give up the ship, run down the colors, and declare the Church an outmoded irrelevancy must be nothing less than a new experience of the power of the Gospel. To see Christ at work in human hearts and lives, to see him bring meaning and purpose to the alienated and purposeless, to witness his power in the forgiveness of sin and the integration of personality through regeneration, is the unanswerable reply to the current mood of despair in which some view the Church.

Now is the time for Protestants who hold the historic biblical faith and who believe in the divine mission and the indestructibility of the Church of Jesus Christ to speak out against the existential blight that oppresses the Body of Christ. We might well ponder these words of Henri-Frederic Amiel in his *Journal Intimé:* "I am oppressed by a feeling of inappropriateness and *malaise* at the sight of philosophy in the pulpit. 'They have taken away my Savior and I know not where they have laid him'; so the simple folk have a right to say and I repeat it with them." Let Protestantism be done with the scandal of self-preoccupation. Let it stop repeating the wearisome clichés of existentialism and get on with fulfilling the commission of its sovereign Lord.

— *Christianity Today,* January 1, 1965

Twenty-Four

WHAT IS THE CHURCH FOR?

What is the Church for? The answer is no mystery. Scripture makes plain that the Church is to be a worshiping body, committed to "show forth the praises of him who hath called [it] out of darkness into his marvellous light"; that it is to proclaim the saving Gospel of Jesus Christ to all the world; and that it is to obey all the teaching of Jesus Christ, its great Head and Lord.

The means whereby the Church may attain these goals are access to God through the work of Christ its Mediator, the Holy Spirit as the source of its power, and the infallible Scriptures as the basis of its instruction.

In this time of uncertainty and confusion about the purpose of the Church, evangelicals as well as liberals need to think clearly. With the zeal for the Gospel reflected in the very word describing them, many evangelicals are saying with deep earnestness, "Let the Church just preach the Gospel, and everything else will be all right." Yet this assertion is inadequate, because it stresses the Church's great priority to the neglect of the other obligations which its Lord places upon it. On the other hand, many liberals are saying, "Let the Church devote itself to political and social reform, and society will be saved." And this is untrue, because it misconceives the jurisdiction of the Church and neglects the Gospel and worship.

Essential to the life and health of the Church is its relationship to God. This depends upon worship, the sacraments or ordinances, and the preaching and hearing of the Word as well as upon service. Speaking to those who make up the "spiritual house" that is the Church, Peter said, "Like living stones be yourselves built into a spiritual house, to be a holy priesthood, to offer spiritual sacrifices acceptable to God through Jesus Christ" (I Pet. 2:5).

It is a valid criticism of both liberalism and evangelicalism that they are long on activism and short on worship. With all their emphasis on social service, liberals need to remember the essentiality of worship; with all their passion for the Gospel, evangelicals must not forget that to adore and praise God is no take-it-or-leave-it matter. We *must* worship God because of who he is. To give him only a careless devotion is to cheat him of his rightful due. Great proclamation of the Gospel, powerful witnessing, Spirit-filled service, cannot be dissociated from true worship of the living God.

But worship does not stand alone. It must be accompanied by obedience to the whole body of Christ's commands. In his Great Commission, the risen Lord said to the disciples to whom he committed responsibility for the building of his Church: "Go therefore and make disciples of all nations, baptizing them in the name of the Father and of the Son and of the Holy Spirit, teaching them to observe all that I have commanded you; and lo, I am with you always, to the close of the age" (Matt. 28:19, 20). Therefore, along with the proclamation of the Gospel leading to discipling and baptizing all nations, the Church is bound to teach those who have been baptized to obey *all* that Christ taught.

At the heart of the Church's mission stands the proclamation of the good news of salvation. But if it does only this and nothing more, it has not been faithful to the whole of its Lord's commission. The Church must also teach and nourish its members, so that they will go out and fulfill their function as "the light of the world" and "the salt of the earth." Christ's commands are clearly set forth in the Gospels and repeated and interpreted in the Epistles. To feed the sheep the Word of God, to care for those in need, to love one's neighbor — to do all these things and others like them in Christ's Name is to obey his teaching. The very structure of the apostolic church provided for Christian humanitarianism; the diaconate (Acts 6:1-6) was begun so that the needy would not be neglected and the apostles would not be diverted from their primary task of preaching and prayer. That this did not mean apostolic indifference is evident from Paul's great concern about the poor in Jerusalem. As he wrote in Galatians, "So then, as we have opportunity, let us do good to all men, and especially to those who are of the household of faith" (6:10).

If liberalism has failed in proclaiming the saving work of Jesus Christ, the reason is that it has rejected the supernatural nature of that work. Yet apart from salvation through Christ's atoning blood and bodily resurrection, worship becomes lifeless formalism; and, apart from the Gospel, social service dwindles to benevolent humanism. Indeed, such service offered as a means of acceptance with God in place of redemption through the Cross insults the God who so loved the world that he gave his Son for its life. Bishop Lesslie Newbigin has rightly said, "There is a terrible danger that the Church should become a large social service organization with its center in a modern streamlined office rather than God's family with its center in 'the apostles' teaching and fellowship, the breaking of bread, and the prayers.'" The New Testament knows nothing of a church devoted to political affairs. The only ecclesiastical proclamation in the New Testament is that of the first-century Jerusalem Council (Acts 15:1-29), and it concerns spiritual matters.

The Church is not a mere organization. It is a living and breathing body. It is made up of imperfect men and women who by grace are enabled to use God's perfect means. The Church that is true to its calling is one in which believers hold fast to God's purpose in saving them. That purpose is set forth by Paul in Ephesians 2:8-10: "By grace you have been saved through faith; and this is not your own doing, it is the gift of God — not because of works, lest any man should boast." If the Church forgets *that,* it has no message, no saving word for a lost world. And if the Church stops with that, it lays itself open to the peril of antinomianism. For the apostle goes on to say *why* God saved us: "We are his workmanship, created in Christ Jesus for good works, which God prepared beforehand, that we should walk in them." While the danger of liberalism is benevolent activity apart from adequate recognition of the one saving Gospel, the danger of evangelicalism is forgetfulness of the essential outcome of the Gospel.

What, then, is the answer to present-day confusion about the purpose of the Church? It is for the Church to strive to be true to "all the counsel of God." It is for the Church to be what God has called it to be — a worshiping community of believers, proclaiming the Gospel of redemption, seeking to observe all things its Lord has commanded it. This, and nothing less than this, is what the Church of Jesus Christ is for.

— *Christianity Today,* September 10, 1965

Twenty-Five
THE MINISTER AND HIS WORK

The work of the ministry is a calling both varied and humbling. After years of training in the Scriptures, in theology, in the discipline of scholarship, and in the understanding of human beings, to be a minister of the Gospel which is "a savor of life unto life and of death unto death" is a task calling a man to daily dependence upon God. Among the complexities of ministerial life and work, four are central: the minister's identity, his concern, his preaching, and his purpose.

Consider first the identity of the minister — who he is as a servant of Christ. According to the Apostle Paul, ministers are men to whom Christ has given special gifts (Eph. 4:7-16). Elementary and higher education are deeply concerned for the training of gifted youth, those students of superior intellectual promise. But in another and different sense the theological seminary also is engaged in the education of the gifted. Paul declares in this passage in Ephesians that the risen, ascended Lord gave particular spiritual gifts to men, so that "some should be apostles, some prophets, some evangelists, some pastors and teachers."

Of these five spiritual gifts, four are present in the Church today. The exception is the gift of apostleship, which was unique with those who had actually seen the Lord himself. But the other gifts have been conferred down through the ages according to Christ's gracious will: the gift of prophecy (no longer the foretelling of the future but rather the speaking forth of rebuke or encouragement, according to God's principles) ; the gift of being an evangelist; and, in indissoluble relation one with the other, the gift of being a pastor and teacher.

In thinking of these gifts and their possession under God, it is a mistake to compartmentalize them rigidly. Undoubtedly

164

all ministers of Christ exercise all four gifts to some degree. But to each our Lord gives in a special measure one or another of the gifts. These gifts are to be thought of not as isolated but as related; and, according to the teaching of the New Testament, every gift is made effective by the one great gift of the Holy Spirit, who indwells every Christian.

It is a wise minister who knows his gift and who cultivates it to the glory of God and the upbuilding of believers. If the Lord has endowed a man as a pastor and teacher, an evangelist, or a prophet, then it is that man's responsibility to develop his gift. Some seminarians may not yet know beyond a doubt what their gifts are, but the Lord who has called them to his service will surely make this plain in the proving ground of experience. And as it becomes plain, they will recognize the appointed field of concentration that is so essential a part of every minister's life.

Consider secondly the concern of the minister. Let us go back in our mind's eye some twenty-five centuries to the situation described in the first chapter of Habakkuk. This man of God, whose book is one of the summits of Old Testament prophecy, lived in the last days of Judah. It was a time much like ours. Habakkuk looked upon the violence and moral corruption and social injustice of his day and cried out to God. The very first sentence of his book shows the prophet's personal concern: He was a man deeply sensitive to what he saw. You will remember that his book opens with these arresting words which stand, as it were, as a title over his writing: "The burden which Habakkuk the prophet did see." (The word translated "burden" means an "oracle" rather than a load.) This man saw the sin and failure of his people. Burdened with the moral problems raised by what he saw, he took these problems to the Lord. Then it was that he received the divine "burden" or "oracle" embodying some of the most profound of all prophetic insights.

Why has God's work gone on through the years? One answer is that there have always been some who, seeing a need, have themselves become involved with it. We should not have the heritage of the Reformed faith had not men like Luther, Calvin, and Knox seen needs and brought them to the Lord. Africa, despite all its problems today, would still be the dark continent it was a century ago had not David Livingstone been burdened to open it for the Gospel. Slavery and child labor would still be practiced in the United States had not concerns been accepted. There would be no progress in race relations were it not for the concerned. Educational institutions have been begun as the result of burdens seen and ·accepted. Seminaries would not exist had not their founders been concerned for training men as pastors and teachers, prophets, or evangelists.

To the young man at the threshold of his work as a minister of Jesus Christ, the challenge is: "Recognize your concern and then bear it in Christ's yoke." Why does a man enter the ministry? "Because God has called me," he answers. But how has God called him? Has it not been through a concern, a sense of the need of men and women for Christ? Moreover, as a man goes on in the ministry, he is continually confronted by new needs and concerns.

It is a principle that a need may under God constitute a call. Our country with its violence and corruption, its God-forgetfulness which we call secularism but which is actually atheism by default, its moral callousness and selfish materialism, its racial prejudice and internal strife, is full of needs and concerns that summon Christians to join what Emile Cailliet calls "the brotherhood of the heavy-laden." Yet basic to all these needs is the need of sinful human beings for the transforming Gospel of Jesus Christ.

As Habakkuk's dialogue with the Lord continued and as the Lord showed him the Babylonian menace on the horizon much like the Communist menace in our day, the prophet complained that the Babylonians were more wicked than Judah. Then it was that Habakkuk went to his watchtower, to a place where he could be alone with God. There God spoke to him and gave him a great message to proclaim.

So we come to a third aspect of the ministry — the work of preaching. Nothing probes personal commitment more deeply than the responsibility of proclaiming God's truth. Are you and I concerned with meeting the needs of men through preaching the Word and proclaiming Christ according to the Scriptures? Then we must first do as Habakkuk did in going apart before

God. At the center of our lives we too must practice being alone with God and waiting upon him. Without this spiritual discipline, no minister, indeed none of us, minister or Christian layman, can be a truly effective witness.

The minister's disciplined continuance in study and scholarship is indispensable. But along with it there goes the inescapable obligation of growing spiritually. The greatest peril to powerful service for Christ is the temptation to neglect the devotional life alone with God. This is a simple truth, but it is nonetheless vital. Out of Habakkuk's waiting upon God came the seven short words, "The just shall live by his faith," that are the germ of the Gospel as the Spirit of God led Paul to expound it in Romans and Galatians. Out of a personal relation with God in prayer and searching the Scriptures come the shaping of the minister's message and strength for proclaiming it.

One of the most remarkable portrayals of preaching is not in any textbook on homiletics but in Herman Melville's *Moby Dick*. One winter Sunday, Ishmael goes to the Whalemen's Church in New Bedford. In a howling storm Father Mapple preaches a sermon on Jonah. But it is the pulpit from which he preaches that interests us. Melville devotes a chapter to it, as he tells how Father Mapple mounts it. It is shaped like the prow of a ship with the Bible on a projection jutting high over the people. It has no stairs, but a rope ladder with red side cords gives access to it. Mapple mounts it with dignity. Then he draws up the ladder after him. There he is, alone in the pulpit. It is an unforgettable picture, rich in symbolism.

Oh, the aloneness, the holy isolation of a man in the pulpit! Who of us preachers has not felt it! Although we do not draw up a ladder after us when we enter the pulpit, we do stand alone and speak to men for God. Yet all the time, by a blessed paradox, we are not alone. Outside Boston's Trinity Episcopal Church there is the great St. Gaudens statue of Phillips Brooks preaching; behind him stands Christ, with his hand on the preacher's shoulder. It is a moving portrayal of the unseen Companion of the faithful minister in the solitude of the pulpit.

The isolation of the pulpit is one of responsibility — the great and inescapable responsibility of declaring the whole counsel of God, of preaching not ourselves but Jesus Christ the Lord, of never substituting the fallible word of man for the infallible Word of God. But though we stand alone before men, paradoxically we must also stand in nearness of mind to mind and heart to heart with those who hear us. The isolation of the pulpit is that of individual responsibility to God for the faithful preaching of his Word; it is not and must never be confused with the isolation that comes from faulty communication.

Perhaps the greatest lack of the evangelical ministry today is failure to proclaim the Gospel clearly. All the orthodoxy the minister holds, all the great body of evangelical truth committed to him, is of little avail unless those who hear him understand the way of salvation through Christ alone and the obligations God places on those who belong to Christ. The problem of preaching is always the problem of communication, and woe to the minister who forgets this.

When Habakkuk waited alone before God, God gave him the answer to his problems and with it this instruction: "Write the vision and make it plain ... that he may run that reads it." God is interested in our making the Gospel plain. We have the message in the unchanging, powerful Gospel of Jesus Christ. It would be well for every minister to resolve never to preach a single sermon without mentioning salvation through Christ. Why? Because there may be someone before him who may never have another opportunity to hear the message of salvation. Always the obligation is to proclaim the redeeming Christ. Paul set the right example when he declared, "I determined not to know anything among you save Jesus Christ and him crucified"; and he was also right when he disclaimed "excellency of speech and of wisdom," which was another way of disclaiming rhetoric for rhetoric's sake.

In a day when philosophy has invaded the pulpit and professional theological jargon obscures basic Christian truth, we need to remember that, aside from the power of the Spirit, the greatest asset a preacher may have is plain speech. The late C. S. Lewis told of a young parson whom he heard close a sermon like this: "My dear friends, if you do not accept this truth, there may be for you grave eschatological consequences." "I asked him," said Dr. Lewis, "if he meant that his hearers would be in danger of going to hell if they didn't believe. And when he said, 'Yes,' I replied, 'Then why didn't you say so?' "

It is significant that among the gifts of Christ to the Church, two are clearly linked — those of "pastors and teachers." To a very real extent preachers *are* teachers. For a preacher there could hardly be any more valuable training than some kind of experience in teaching. Such experience is important simply because the good teacher must constantly ask himself: "Am I making this plain? Are my students understanding this? How can I make this point more clear?," questions the preacher ought to ask of every sermon he preaches.

Few ministers will be college or seminary professors, but no minister can escape being an essential part of the great enterprise of Christian education. This means that preaching that expounds the Word of God is not optional but obligatory. A question that every preacher ought to face as he takes stock of his ministry year by year is not just, "Have my people been inspired and challenged?," but, "Do they know more about the Bible than they did last year?" For through the Bible we know more of Christ.

The good teacher must know his pupils — not just their names, but their backgrounds and what interests them and what they are thinking. So with the pastor-teacher. He cannot make himself understood unless he understands the cultural environment of his hearers. The godly isolation of the pulpit does not mean lack of cultural awareness. Evangelicalism has been making great strides in overcoming anti-intellectualism, but it has far to go in overcoming cultural provincialism. For effective communication of the Gospel the minister must speak to people where they are — not just on Sunday morning but where they are every day in their interests and thoughts and recreation.

The fourth aspect of the ministry — namely, its purpose — may be stated with urgent brevity. Some of you have been given spiritual gifts, Paul is saying in Ephesians 4:7-16, and you have been given these gifts for a purpose. That purpose is both broad and wonderful. As the New English Bible correctly translates

Paul's words: "These were his gifts: some to be apostles, some prophets, some evangelists, some pastors and teachers, [and now note the purpose] to equip God's people for work in his service." And, Paul continues, "so shall we all at last attain to the unity inherent in our faith and our knowledge of the Son of God — to mature manhood, measured by nothing less than the full stature of Christ."

Every minister should be careful of an overly exclusive view of his ministry. Yes, he is a man specially endowed. By ordination he is set apart. He has special functions such as preaching and pastoral care and the administration of the sacraments. But the purpose of it all is that as pastor and teacher he should help the rank and file of believers exercise *for themselves* the work of the ministry in the unity and maturity of truth and love. The test of the minister's exercise of his gift is the growth into maturity of those entrusted to his pastoral care and instruction. And mature Christians we must have! The moral and spiritual flabbiness of undernourished, underdeveloped church members cannot stand up to the pressures of this secular age.

There are indeed various aspects of the ministry; Christ gives men different gifts. But the foundation and central point of reference to which all else (evangelism included) is related, the purpose always to be kept in mind and heart in the work of the ministry, is nothing less than the growth and unity of the body of Christ unto mature manhood, even unto the full stature of Christ.

Commencement address, Calvin Theological Seminary and Fuller Theological Seminary, 1964.

— *Christianity Today,* January 1, 1965

Twenty-Six

WHAT IS TRUTH?

No question has more insistently laid hold upon the minds of men than the three words at the head of this essay. They are forever associated with Pilate, not because he was the first to ask them, but because he spoke them face to face with the most important person who ever lived, and spoke them, moreover, on the most crucial day of human history. There, in the judgment hall in Jerusalem, sat Pontius Pilate, Roman Governor of Judea; before him stood Jesus Christ, outwardly a prisoner, but mighty in the dignity of truth. As the inquiry proceeded, Pilate said, "Art thou a king then?"

To Pilate's question, Jesus replied, "Thou sayest that I am a king. To this end was I born, and for this cause came I into the world, that I should bear witness to the truth. Everyone that is of the truth heareth my voice." Whereupon the Governor — not, we may be sure, a "jesting Pilate," despite Bacon's famous phrase — asked, "What is truth?"

From the beginning, human philosophy has been occupied with the answer to this question. Science seeks to discover truth in the natural realm; art and literature try to express it in portraying the world and life; education and religion strive to identify and explicate it. The common man, when he thinks about the meaning of life and death and the world, as all men sometimes do, is asking the same question. It is a query that nobody, least of all a student living in these troubled times, can possibly evade.

Can it be answered? And if a Christian replies, "Yes, it can," some important implications have to be faced. There is, for example, the seeming assumption that an ordinary, everyday person who is neither a philosopher, scientist, creative artist, nor theologian, is claiming to know what the greatest minds have

171

failed to find out. "Do you mean to tell us," someone says, "that you know what truth, the essential truth of all things, really is? Surely, you don't expect to be taken seriously. After all, Christians are supposed to be humble."

But a believing man does expect to be taken seriously when he claims knowledge of the truth. The plain fact is that this plausible talk about presumption and lack of humility is beside the point. No believer in his right mind even begins to say that he has for the first time discovered or found out the truth that is at the heart of all things. What he does say is something quite different — that the truth has been revealed, that by the grace of God his eyes have been opened to it, and that, far from being a discoverer or originator of the truth, he is but a witness to it. Thus the presumption lies not in proclaiming the truth but in keeping quiet about it. For to keep quiet about it implies one of three things: either that one is afraid to acknowledge it, or that it is not true after all, or else that it is not worth asserting. The first alternative is cowardly; the other two insulting. And to deal like this with truth is presumption in the nth degree. Let it not be forgotten that, while great minds have failed in their own wisdom to find the truth, other intellects of the stature of an Augustine or a Pascal, to say nothing of a Paul, have known it by faith and have dedicated heart and life to its proclamation.

What, then, is truth? The foregoing, with its emphasis upon knowledge through faith, points to the answer. Truth in its underlying aspect — that is, truth in its essence — is not made or originated by man but revealed to man. This is to state the answer in general terms. But when it comes to the age-old query of the human spirit, generalities are not in themselves enough. We turn again, therefore, to the scene in Pilate's judgment hall. When the Governor said to Jesus, "What is truth?" he had before him the answer, though he did not know it. Facing him was the only person among the world's great religious leaders who could say and who did say of himself with complete assurance, "I am ... the truth." Not only that, but if we go back just a few hours, we find that in his prayer on the way to Gethsemane Jesus said to his Father, "Thy word is truth." So the answer to Pilate's question is this: Jesus Christ himself is the truth; Scripture is truth.

Let us look hard at these two propositions in the endeavor to find out whether they really tell us what truth is. As we do this, we must first of all take a moment to refresh ourselves about how we recognize something as being true. In other words, we need to inquire into what the truthfulness of truth is.

Who of us, on being suddenly confronted with some startling piece of news, has not exclaimed, "Is it really true?" Now it is the adverb in this colloquialism that points to the test of the truth. The reason is simply that, when we ask whether a thing is "really" true, we are, almost unconsciously, invoking the criterion of correspondence with reality. Whether it be a matter of science like Einstein's epoch-making equation, E equals MC^2; or whether it be a particular virtue in the intangible realm of character, such as that a certain man is courageous, correspondence with reality is the criterion of the truthfulness of truth. In the former instance, scientific experiment shows the equation to be in accord with physical reality; in the latter instance, demonstrated bravery in fear-producing circumstances validates courage.

What has just been said represents common ground between believer and unbeliever; all of us, Christian and non-Christian alike, admit that reality is the test of truth. While in respect to the nature of reality there are great differences, there is general agreement about the necessity for whatever is claimed to be true to correspond with reality.

With these things in mind, we look more deeply into the answer to Pilate's question. As we have already seen, that answer tells us that Christ is truth and that the Word of God is truth. But no sooner are these propositions stated than a dissent is heard. "Hold on," we are told, "how can you identify one man with truth? And do you actually expect the modern mind to swallow the assumption that a single book, written in ancient, pre-scientific times, is the everlasting truth?"

Formidable as these objections sound, they need not frighten us. After all, there are perfectly good answers to them. In the first place, we can identify one man with truth, provided that we know that one man to be Jesus Christ and provided that we know who Jesus Christ really is. In the second place, we have a perfect right to declare a book, even though written long before this modern era, to be the truth, provided that we are dealing with a divinely inspired book.

To go back to the first objection, a moment's reflection shows that it rests upon an inadequate view of Jesus Christ. It begs the question by presupposing that he was no more than a man. Grant its premise, and its logic is unassailable, because it is quite true that no mere man can possibly be in himself all the truth. But the premise need not be granted; the central place of Jesus Christ in human history, the centuries-long expectation for a deliverer like him, his stupendous claim to be more than a man, his perfect life and his unique death with its equally unique sequel, his continuing power over the human heart during a period of nearly two thousand years — these are facts corresponding with verifiable historical reality. Taken together, they can be explained only on the ground that Christ was what he said he was and what the New Testament asserts him to be, deity manifest in human form, the God-man, perfect in humanity, fully God in deity.

Christ, then, is the truth, because, human though he was, through his deity he was and is at the same time an infinite person. Not only that, but any adequate conception of God must also hold that deity is the ultimate reality of all things.

Can one person be big enough to be the truth? In reply, we need only say, "Consider Jesus Christ." Fully man though he was, he is at the same time God. Therefore, it follows that to ask whether Christ is big enough to be the truth is the same thing as asking whether God is big enough to be the truth, a question that answers itself. Moreover, the criterion of truth is, as has already been shown, correspondence with reality. Now if God is the ultimate reality of all things, and if Christ is God as well as man, then Christ only among men is the truth, because he alone is reality.

All Christians accept Jesus as God; they would not be Christians if they did not do so. But not all Christians realize the implications of this momentous affirmation. How much it means, Robert Browning tells us in *A Death in the Desert:*

> *I say, the acknowledgment of God in Christ*
> *Accepted by thy reason, solves for thee*
> *All questions in the earth and out of it,*
> *And has so far advanced thee to be wise.*

It is one thing to believe as an article of the creed that Jesus Christ is God; it is another thing consistently to place his deity at the center of one's thought and life. A book by J. B. Phillips bears the title, *Your God Is Too Small.* After showing the inadequacy of a number of the commonly held ideas of God, the author shows that God in Christ is alone big enough for the great issues of life and death and eternity. The trouble is that many Christians, though professing faith in the infinite Son of God, have in actuality but a limited conception of his greatness. Thinking of him as exclusively a religious figure, they dwarf him to the confines of a particular church, to some man-made creed, or to the observance of one day out of seven.

But he is too big for that. In his greatness, he comprehends all the past, the whole present, and the entire future. There is nothing in the universe to which, directly or indirectly, he does not bear some relationship. For as John, referring to Christ as "the Word," expressed it in the prologue to his Gospel: "In the beginning was the Word, and the Word was with God, and the Word was God. The same was in the beginning with God. All things were made by him, and without him was not anything made that was made. In him was life; and the life was the light of men." To take seriously the profundities of these words and really to think about them is to see something of the universal relevance of the Lord Jesus Christ.

We turn now to the second proposition with which Pilate's question is answered — namely, that Scripture is truth. Said the Lord Jesus in the most solemn and exalted prayer ever uttered, "Thy word is truth," thus equating with truth Scripture, which is the revelation of himself, the incarnate Word. In the face of his authority and in the light of what Scripture really is, the objection that an ancient book written by "unenlightened" men before the advent of modern science cannot be the truth falls to the ground. It is not theories of biblical inspiration that validate the written Word of God; it is the Book itself with its eternally contemporary setting forth of the everlasting verities. As no other writing in all the world, it brings Jesus Christ to men. Despite its diversity of human authorship and variety of contents, it is a unit in that, from beginning to end, it communicates the life-giving truth of Christ. No other book is plainer in its down-to-earth portrayal of human life; none more exalted in its insistence upon the reality of the eternal. On the one hand, it shows us what men are here and now; on the other hand, it points behind the things of the world to the abiding reality of the invisible, telling us that "the things which are seen are temporal; but the things which are not seen are eternal."

Because it is the Word of God, communicating the Son of God to men, the dimensions of the Bible are more than finite. The only Book that really begins at the beginning, it opens in eternity with God and answers the question, "Where did all things come from?" The only Book that actually ends at the end of history, it closes with the centrality of Christ in the new heaven and the new earth and answers the question, "What will the consummation of all things be?"

At this point, we hear still another objection. "All this about the infinite nature of Christ and the eternal scope of the Bible sounds good in principle. But let us get down to facts," someone says. "We live in a world of science and industry, a world of jet planes and space travel, movies and television, psychiatry and antibiotics, atonalism and surrealism, pragmatism and existentialism, Communism and democracy. What has the latter part of this twentieth century got to do with Christ and the Bible?"

It is a relevant question, and honesty requires that it be answered. More than that, it brings us straight up against what may well be the most important principle in Christian thought, or, for that matter, in any kind of thought at all. That principle is the continuity of all truth under God. Or, to put it in other words, it is the principle that all truth — whether in religion or philosophy, science or art, industry or politics — is God's truth. In the light of this principle, the conventional schism between secular truth and sacred truth is wrong. Every truth, no matter in what realm of life it may be found, is of God and under God. There may, to be sure, be different orders of truth, such as truth discoverable by man in chemistry or mathematics, as compared with revealed truth. Yet the different orders of truth are continuous and complementary, not discontinuous and contradictory.

Moreover, there is an order of truth — namely, that which is revealed because man cannot discover it — which is known only through Christ and the Bible. This is not to say that the whole of the Bible is revealed truth, which is obviously not the case, since there is in Scripture plenty of truth on the historical and natural level. But it is to say that truth of the order of revelation is exclusive with Christ and the Bible.

In the light of these undeniable principles, what are we to say, for example, of the tremendous increase of particular aspects of scientific truth so characteristic of the modern world? How does knowledge of this kind fit into the truth set forth in the Word of God? Well, first of all we must acknowledge that, when it comes to specific technical terms, the Bible tells us nothing. In respect to the equations of atomic physics or colloidal chemistry, it is silent. Of the intricacies of guided missiles, it says no more than it does of the latest trends in modern music. Nor is there any need for it to speak in such technicalities. The all-important fact is that it provides the framework within which all true knowledge, ancient as well as modern, fits as part of God's overall truth. Not only that, but it also sets forth the essential moral and spiritual absolutes, the eternal checks and balances, without which the whole vast expansion of modern science is a Pandora's box, threatening the survival of civilized man.

The fact, so tragically forgotten in a world that pays but lip-service to the Son of God, is that only in subordination to him who "is before all things" and by whom "all things consist [hold together]" can any truth, whether in science or mathematics, literature or sociology, attain its real significance. Divorced from him, it is not only transitory and incomplete; it may also become

177

a potential menace to the well-being of a humanity created in the image of the eternal Reality, who is God.

Our inquiry has led us into an exposition of the Christian view of truth. But the Bible is a book of action rather than analysis, and Christ is a Lord to be followed rather than merely admired. The truth of God, unlike the truth of the philosophers, lays upon humanity an obligation not to be evaded. As F. W. Robertson said, "He is already half false who speculates on truth and does not do it. Truth is given, not to be contemplated but to be done. Life is an action — not a thought."

This being the case, we must conclude by facing what it means to do the truth. Here, as in every instance where Scripture lays an obligation upon man, we are not left in any doubt. The words of Christ that led to Pilate's memorable question tell us exactly what is meant by doing the truth. For, on being interrogated about his kingship, Christ had replied: "Thou sayest that I am a king. To this end was I born, and for this cause came I into the world, that I should bear witness unto the truth."

Now if any man can be said to have done the truth, that man was Jesus Christ. When Christ in his humanity stood before Pilate and when Pilate exclaimed to the hostile multitude, "Behold, the man," he spoke better than he knew. Christ was the only man of perfect integrity the world has ever seen. And his integrity was epitomized by his relation to the truth.

Doing the truth means doing just what Christ did — bearing witness to it. As for bearing witness to the truth, it is more than a matter of words, though it necessarily includes verbal testimony. Christ alone among men was the perfect witness, because he himself was wholly true. His life was wholly true in its complete conformity with his Father's will. Contrary to some modern interpreters, Christ never claimed to have discovered or originated the truth. It was not through his own spiritual insights that he "became" the Son of God; rather was it because he was the Son that the Father committed to him all truth. Therefore, it was his mission in his humanity to bear witness to that truth. This he did in his teaching, in his life, and in his death and resurrection. Everything about Christ — every word, every deed, even the thought behind the word and the deed — was a witness to the truth.

So it must be with Christians, apart from the immeasurable gap between perfection and human striving. We are not witnesses in the sense that we have found out for ourselves the truth which is eternal reality. On the contrary, it is because we are regenerate sons of God through faith in Christ that the truth is committed to us. Said our Lord to his Father: "As thou hast sent me into the world, even so have I also sent them into the world." Therefore, our mission is, like that of Christ, to bear witness to the truth and to be committed in mind and heart and life to the will of God, to have as the criterion of every word and act nothing less than conformity with the truth; thus to make Christ known in word and deed — this is what is meant by bearing witness to the truth.

— *His,* April, 1954

Twenty-Seven
WHY THE BIBLE?

Some of the greatest things are the least appreciated, simply because they are so well known. As Goethe said, "If the rainbow stood for a day, no one would look at it." This tendency to take the familiar for granted applies to many things, including books as well as the beauties of nature.

In all honesty, there are very few of us who have wholly escaped the self-deception of persuading ourselves that we know some great book everybody is supposed to know, although in point of fact we have never really gotten round to reading it. And so it is worth while just to stop now and then and ask some plain questions about some of the great things we take for granted.

Robert Vogeler, an American official of the International Telephone and Telegraph Company employed in Hungary, was seized by the Communists and, despite strong protest by our government, was imprisoned. On his release, he described the torment of solitary confinement and told how his captors finally let him have a Bible in his cell. "When my request for a Bible was granted," said Vogeler, "I treated it as one treats a priceless possession, a thing of great value, a rare treasure.... It gave me," he said, "strength and assurance for what, to my knowledge at that time, were the interminable years ahead."

But why the Bible? Why didn't Robert Vogeler beg the Communists to let him have a copy of Shakespeare or Browning, or perhaps of Faulkner or Hemingway? Why the Bible?

The same question emerges out of an incident related by Major General Courtney Whitney in his book entitled *MacArthur's Rendezvous with History*. The night before the landing at Inchon, Courtney Whitney and his chief were aboard the flagship *Mt. McKinley* in the Yellow Sea. Whitney had been asleep only a short time when he was called to MacArthur's cabin. He found the General, in bathrobe and slippers, pacing the floor, and in a kind of self-debate, talking as he paced. One by one he reviewed the arguments against the landing and countered with reasons for the surprise attack. At last, at two-thirty in the morning, he concluded by saying that he believed the decision was sound.

"Thanks for listening to me," he said. "Now let's get some sleep." Whereupon, the writer adds, "he threw off his robe, climbed into bed and reached to the table alongside to pick up his Bible."

Again we ask: Why the Bible? Why was this Book there? Why did this great commander on the eve of a momentous action turn, as many another commander before him has turned and as you some day may turn, to his Bible?

I think we may say that men turn to the Bible in preference to any other book because, as Professor Cailliet of Princeton says, "The Book of books does not belong to a realm, if by realm a class is meant. The Bible is not in a class. It constitutes a class by itself."

We see, then, that it is really with the uniqueness of Scripture that we have to do. And in order that we may understand its uniqueness I give you three propositions. The first comes from Psalm 119, where the writer says: "The entrance of thy words giveth light" (v. 130) ; the second is in John 17:17, where Christ declares: "Thy word is truth"; and the third is from the same Gospel, John 5:39, where he says: "Search the Scriptures; for in them ye think ye have eternal life: and they are they which testify of me." Each of the propositions gives us a definite answer to the question, Why the Bible?

The first answer is that the Bible is unique because, in a sense that applies to no other book in the world, it enlightens us. "The entrance of thy words giveth light."

Someone has put it in this simple illustration. Imagine, if you will, a father and his small son in the midst of a dense and remote forest (in such terrain as that in which I recently spent time camping in the Rocky Mountains of British Columbia) . The father, who is about to go away, impresses the boy with his danger. There are wild animals. The temperature will go below freezing before morning. There is no food. But there is a place of warmth and food and shelter, if only the boy can find it.

"Father, show me how to get there," the boy asks.

"No," comes the reply, "find it yourself."

"But give me a light for my feet."

"No, I will not."

"Then, Father, just draw me a map; maybe I can read it by the light of the moon."

"No."

Imagine such a father! Yet that is what God would be like, had he left us without a revelation to guide us in this world. Why the Bible? It is the divine guidebook for the journey which you and I, and all men, are making — this pilgrimage of life through the years on to our eternal destiny.

Now let us be perfectly sure that we understand exactly what we mean by calling the Bible the guidebook. We are not speaking in a mundane sense only. Scripture is not just a textbook of science or of history. When it deals with these things, it speaks factually and truly, although sometimes figuratively and poetically. But its main function concerns the heart and the conscience and the soul of man as well as his mind and body. As Galileo said, "The Bible was given not to tell us how the heavens go, but to tell us how to go to heaven." So the Bible lights our way. It can do this, because it is the only book that is fully identified with truth.

This brings us to our second answer. We turn to the Bible in preference to all other books, just because it is truth. When you want reliable information about a subject, you go, if you are wise, to the highest authority. And when it comes to matters of conscience and when you want to know about God, the one supreme authority is Jesus Christ.

So we go to him and hear him say of God's written revelation: "Thy word is truth." Not —"Thy word contains truth"; not —"Thy word leads to truth"; but, categorically —"Thy word *is* truth." Thus did Jesus Christ equate Scripture with the truth of the living God.

For here in the Bible is the only true landscape of reality. Here is the one eternally true frame of reference. Here is the blazing truth about man, revealing the human heart with its sin and rebellion against God, and the word of redemption through his Son. Here is the truth about history and the nations, set down with the awful candor of the Judge of all the earth. Here is the truth about you and me, the laying bare of the secrets of our hearts and lives, and the help and strength and forgiveness we need day by day as well as in times of crisis.

Yes, the Bible is truth, as our Lord said. But it is vital for you and me to see that it is truth of a particular order. It is not abstract truth, but truth related to a Person. Said our Lord to a group of religionists in Jerusalem who denied his mission: "Search the Scriptures...for they are they which testify of me."

Why the Bible? There is, then, a third answer to this question. This is it: in Scripture, truth is made known in a Person, so that in a very special sense the whole Bible bears witness to the Lord Jesus Christ. Beyond its moral precepts, greater than its laws, even above its devotional teaching is the fact that it gives us the Gospel. And the Gospel, as someone said, "is good news, not good advice." What is that good news? It is nothing less than the proclamation that God loves the world, that God gave his only Son for the world, that in the death of his Son on the cross God has done for us what we could never do for ourselves — he has forgiven our sins and made all who believe in him new men in Christ.

During the First World War President Woodrow Wilson said: "No man is indispensable." Humanly speaking, he was right. But humanly speaking is not biblically speaking, as Woodrow Wilson, himself a Christian believer, would have been the first to admit. In the biblical sense, and therefore in the truest sense, there is but one man who is indispensable, the Man Christ Jesus.

Why the Bible? Because if it had never been written, we should be ignorant of this Man who accomplished the most indispensable work in history.

After the Napoleonic wars, Talleyrand, it is said, was struggling with the problem of European reconstruction. A young man said to him with great enthusiasm: "Sir, what Europe needs is a new religion that will be suited to this new day."

The astute diplomat listened, as the enthusiast explained his recipe for reconstruction. Then he replied: "My young man, if you feel it is time for a new religion, go out in the highways and byways and begin to elucidate your principles; only be sure that you incorporate them perfectly in your own conduct. Then, when you have done that, lay down your life for the people and, after you are buried three days, return from the dead and share that victory with your followers."

And Talleyrand might have added, had he known more of true Christianity: "In doing all these things, make sure that they had already been set down hundreds of years before in a book by men who had never heard of you; and make sure also that, after you did them, your followers would write about you in a sequel to that book with such power that the world would never stop reading it."

So, the question, Why the Bible? has brought us to him whom the Book is all about. This fact — that Jesus Christ is the center of the Bible — is no more debatable than that he is the center of the ages. In either case, it is a plain matter of history.

But true as this is, the greatest mistake any of us can make about the Bible is to take its central character as only an historical figure. He is infinitely more. Of all the great of the past, he alone conquered death. In a sense that belongs only to him, he is living now. The living Christ is not a denominational figure; no church or sect can claim exclusive possession of him. He is greater than all our human systems, and to know him is life eternal.

Therefore, the reading of your Bible lays a very special claim upon you. You read any book and you form your opinion of it. And that's that. If your opinion is favorable, you may reread the book. If the book offers advice, you may take the advice. But there is no book by man, no matter how great his genius, that has a binding claim upon your soul.

The Bible is different — utterly different. Though written by men, and in that sense a human book, it is in origin and inspiration exactly what Christ said it was — the Word of God, the

Word of truth. Thus it lays a unique claim upon you. For God must be obeyed; his words must be done.

In the Bible he speaks to your mind and heart, but most especially to your will. There is no such thing in the religion of the Bible as a merely objective take-it-or-leave-it, standing-on-the-sidelines attitude in matters of faith. God requires decision of every man. The great question is still the one asked long ago by Pilate: "What shall I do then with Jesus who is called Christ?"

For the Bible, you see, is the most personal of books. In it God is speaking directly to you and to me. It is, in fact, a message from God personally addressed to every man.

The mere fact that a Bible is presented and accepted (or acquired in some other way), does not mean that this Bible will fulfill its purpose. An unread Bible is an ineffectual Bible. In the Book as a mere physical object, there is no virtue. Despite the stories of Bibles in soldiers' pockets stopping bullets, Scripture is not a protective charm. It is the book of God's truth, and you and I are obligated to read it and believe it.

What does this mean for us? Just this — we are to read our Bible with an open mind and a receptive heart, to acknowledge the truth of what it says about our need and our sin (for it has something to say about these things to us today as it has spoken to men in all ages) ; to give up, once and for all, the impossible effort of saving ourselves by the good we do; and to put our trust now and forever in Jesus Christ. And then, having done that, we are to undertake the plain duty of going on in daily obedience to him whom to know is life eternal.

A sermon delivered in the Chapel of the United States Military Academy at West Point, New York, at the 86th Annual Presentation of Bibles to the Fourth Classmen by the American Tract Society, September, 1955.
— *Moody Monthly*, February, 1956

Twenty-Eight
LET'S RETURN TO GOD'S WORD

One of the major problems of Protestantism today is the biblical illiteracy of the laity. "I dreamed," said John Bunyan at the beginning of his great allegory, "and behold I saw a man clothed with rags standing in a certain place . . . a book in his hand, and a great burden upon his back."

If John Bunyan were writing today, he would have to describe Christian differently. Man is still a pilgrim; but now he stands in a situation unknown to Bunyan, surrounded, as Pascal prophetically said, by "those frightful spaces of the universe," of which science has made him more aware than ever before. Christian no longer holds the book in his hand, because he does not take it seriously.

Let ministers give their congregations the most elementary tests of scriptural knowledge and ponder the results. By a strange paradox, Bibles are purchased in all manner of versions. They may indeed be read — sporadically and piecemeal. But of the Book as a whole, of its grand unfolding of God's truth and of its essential doctrines, there is a dearth of knowledge.

Why should this be? The answer points to the Church. If at a time when church membership in America is at a high level a living knowledge of the Bible is declining among the laity, the Church must be held accountable for its educational stewardship.

Books are essential to education, and at the heart of Christian education is *the* Book. But something has happened in Protestantism that has immeasurably weakened the hold of Scripture upon the people. There has been a shift in attitude toward the Bible. Liberal scholarship that dissects major portions of Scripture and denies much of the supernaturalism of the Bible has for decades so confidently acclaimed its conjectures as "the assured results of scientific criticism" that they have been accepted by the common man as a *fait accompli*. Despite growing archaeological evidence, rationalistic higher criticism has refused to acknowledge its mistakes. Superimposed upon this unrepentant liberalism is the contemporary tendency to demythologize the Bible in order to accommodate it to this age of science. "Biblicist" has become a pejorative epithet for those holding a conservative view of Scripture. "The Word of God" as an acceptable designation of the Bible is now rejected by many on the ground that this term refers only to the incarnate Word. And this despite Scripture's own repeated designation of itself as the Word of God! Through the publicizing of critical views of the Bible (witness the recent article in *Life* magazine), the faith of the laity in God's Word written has been shaken. Sunday school curricula in leading denominations divest Scripture of the authority of its self-witness, an authority attested by Christ himself and held by the Fathers and the Reformers.

But liberalism is not alone in its unsatisfactory teaching of Scripture. If insisting upon the mechanics of JEDP and if equating critical conjecture about the Bible with fact have broken down faith in the authority of the Bible, honesty demands that conservatives take a fresh look at *their* Bible teaching. In too many evangelical schools and colleges the Bible department is comparatively weak. The fault lies in a pedestrian instruction that forgets that loyalty to high doctrine and to scriptural authority does not preclude exciting teaching of the Bible. Indeed, over-dogmatism that hands to the inquiring student the deep things of God all wrapped up in neat parcels, that insists upon the letter and too often forgets the spirit, does not lead to vital personal use of God's Word. If it is a crime against literature to teach Shakespeare on a dull level of mediocrity, it is a far greater crime to combine doctrinal soundness with lifeless Bible teaching. Yet inadequate as some conservative teaching of the Bible is, it at least produces a larger share of biblical literacy than the more liberal peripheral methods that fail to impart even the simplest facts about the Scriptures.

The consequences of all this are disappointing. In a forthright article in *Theological Education* (Autumn, 1964), Professor John Bright of Union Theological Seminary (Richmond) says of seminary students today: "The typical student has come from a Christian home, has attended the church school from childhood, has come through the communicants' class, perhaps has been active in youth work and attended youth conferences. Quite likely, he has gone to a denominational college where Bible is required, and perhaps has even taken a major in religion. Yet he doesn't know the simplest facts of Biblical history and content. It is all too common to find a student who is glib in the latest theological fashions — who can discourse on *Heilsgeschichte, Formgeschichte,* and *Entmythologisierung,* on Bultmann and Tillich — but who can't tell you with any precision who King David was, or what Isaiah or Jeremiah had to say. The whole structure of theological education (at least in Biblical studies) has sunk a story into the mud of ignorance for want of a foundation."

Something has gone very wrong in Protestant Bible teaching. So fearful have many scholars become of the "paper Pope" bugbear that they have lost the classical Protestant reliance upon the Word of God. Moreover, they have communicated this loss to the people, so that for many Scripture has ceased to be the daily bread for men's souls. And why should it be, if it is in good part mythical, unhistoric, and so far out of keeping with superior modern knowledge as is alleged? Only the man who cares enough for the Bible to read it daily, to hide it in his heart, to rest his very soul upon its truth, and to live by its precepts is the man who takes it seriously.

This is not a plea for a wooden literalism that believes all words of Scripture to be equally important, that fails to distinguish between what is symbolical and poetical, doctrinal and practical, and that considers the writers of Scripture mere automata rather than human beings whose talents God sovereignly used. On the contrary, it is still possible to recognize the human element in Scripture and at the same time hold with intellectual integrity a high view of the Bible as the infallible, authoritative Word of the living God and the indispensable sourcebook of Christian faith and practice. If man today is to stand with the Book once more in his hand — and how desperately he needs thus to stand — he must be brought back to respect for the integrity and authority of the Bible.

It is ironical that at a time when Roman Catholicism is recovering the Bible for the laity, Protestantism should be losing its Bible. Along with our fascinated preoccupation with renewal in Rome, we Protestants need to set ourselves to the task of biblical renewal within our own house.

The direction of that renewal is plain. It lies in a return to the central principle of education — namely, that of going to the original sources. For Christianity *the* sourcebook is the Bible. What is demanded is to put aside secondary sources and teach the people the Bible itself. It will take humility to admit this, but the modern Sunday school curriculum follows a method that would not be tolerated in an accredited school or college. In secular education the day is long past when literature was taught from textbooks about authors without reading more than mere snippets of their works.

Protestantism began in biblical renewal. If it has to a large extent lost its Bible, let it return to the Book that made it great. Let layman and minister alike become once more men with the Book in their hands.

— *Christianity Today,* February 26, 1965

Twenty-Nine

THE CONTINUING POWER
OF THE RESURRECTION

The resurrection of Jesus Christ along with his crucifixion is unique among the countless events of human history. The Lord who left the garden tomb empty is personally present in our time just as he has been personally present in every generation since he "died for our sins according to the scriptures ... was buried, and ... rose again the third day according to the scriptures" (I Cor. 15:3, 4). The resurrection is essential historical fact. Among the things that set it apart from every other miracle is its day-by-day, continuing reality. And it is significant of its abiding power that of all the great Christian festivals, the resurrection has had not one but fifty-two yearly observances ever since the infant Church began to meet for worship on the first, or Lord's Day, instead of on the Jewish Sabbath.

The biography of R. W. Dale, the English theologian, tells how, well on in his public ministry, he "made the discovery that Jesus was alive," and it transformed everything for him. To know the living Lord is for the on-going Christian life indispensable. When the risen Saviour appeared to the disciples in the locked room that first Easter night and spoke of his death and resurrection, he said to them, "You are witnesses of these things" (Luke 24:48). Likewise we who "have not seen, and yet have believed" (John 20:29) are also witnesses of his death and resurrection.

"But how," it may be asked, "is it possible today to be a witness of that which took place nearly two thousand years ago?" The answer lies in the New Testament teaching about the identification of the Christian with his Lord.

Nowhere is this truth more explicitly stated than in Paul's epistles. Like a golden thread, it runs through his exposition of the Christian life in Romans, Corinthians, Galatians, Ephesians, and Colossians. Its logic is this: the believer is identified with Christ in his death and resurrection. "For if we have been united with him in a death like his, we shall certainly be united with him in a resurrection like his. . . . But if we have died with Christ, we believe that we shall also live with him." So Paul declares in the sixth chapter of Romans (5, 8). And at the beginning of the third chapter of Colossians, he puts the fact of the union of the believer with the risen Lord in words of lofty beauty: "If ye then be risen with Christ, seek those things which are above. . . . For ye are dead, and your life is hid with Christ in God" (1, 3); while in Galatians the truth sounds out like a trumpet, as Paul boldly says: "I am crucified with Christ: nevertheless I live; yet not I, but Christ liveth in me . . ." (2:20).

The Christian's witness to the resurrection of Jesus Christ is more than a matter of apologetics. To say this is not to belittle the value of a careful study and faithful presentation of the biblical and historical evidences for this stupendous miracle. Such study is essential; but it can never be a substitute for that personal identification of the believer with his risen Lord which the New Testament presents as the very norm for Christian experience.

In speaking of union with Christ in his death and resurrection, Paul is not talking about some special, esoteric experience available only to an inner circle of ultra-pious members of the Church. On the contrary, he is teaching the very basis of spiritual experience that normally belongs to the heritage of every Christian. That most profound of Negro spirituals goes to the heart of this truth as it asks the haunting questions, "Were you there when they crucified my Lord? Were you there when they nailed him to the tree? Were you there when they laid him in the tomb?" To these words of the original might well be added the further question, "Were you there when he rose up from the tomb?"

It is, however, a disquieting fact that what for Paul was normal Christian experience is comparatively little understood among church members today. And often when it is recognized, this normative truth becomes the subject of a "Deeper" or

191

"Victorious Life" Conference, apart from the ordinary life of the Church. Nevertheless, this truth is for all Christians, young and old. Inseparably linked to the fact of the resurrection, it assures the believer of power for daily living through obedient submission to the living Christ who dwells in his heart by faith.

Perhaps therein lies the seed of its neglect. The price of submission is not small. It costs nothing less than the freedom to run one's own life — a price many are unwilling to pay in a day when self-fulfillment is exalted as the ultimate goal.

In an Easter sermon, a leading preacher said, "We are afraid of the empty tomb. It brings up all sorts of questions that we would not like to have to answer." But why should Christians who believe God be afraid of the empty tomb? To be sure, they may not understand all about it. God clothed in mystery what happened within it. No man saw the Son of God arise. His death was for all to see, his resurrection hidden from every human eye. Alice Meynell speaks of its holy privacy in these lines:

> *Public was Death; but Power, but Might,*
> *But Life again, but Victory,*
> *Were hushed within the dead of night,*
> *The shutter'd dark, the secrecy.*
> *And all alone, alone, alone,*
> *He rose again behind the stone.*[1]

Yet though the manner of Christ's rising is known only to God, it is the prerogative of Christians to be certain of its fact. Therefore, instead of fearing the empty tomb, they should rejoice in it as the sign of victory over empty and defeated lives.

Moreover, this victory is meant to be realized in the dust and heat of everyday living. Paul leaves no doubt that the truth of the believer's identification with the risen Christ has its earthly application as well as its heavenly assurance of personal resurrection, when the believer's longing to be "clothed upon" will be satisfied in a body like unto Christ's glorious body. At the end of the seventh chapter of Romans, the Apostle describes the

---

[1] From "Easter Night" in *The Poems of Alice Meynell*. London: Oxford University Press, 1940.

tensions inside human personality with a precision anticipative of the insights of modern psychology. "For that which I do, I allow not: for what I would, that do I not; but what I hate, that do I..." (Rom. 7:15). Then, having dissected the hopelessness of the anguished struggle, he exclaims, "Who shall deliver me from the body of this death?" (v. 24). Whereupon he shows in the glorious eighth chapter that through the risen Christ who indwells the believer there is victory indeed. Similarly in Colossians, after reminding Christians of their identification with their living Lord ("If ye then be risen with Christ..."), he speaks with plain practicality about mortifying and putting off the sins of the body and spirit and putting on the great virtues of love and forbearance (Col. 3:1-15).

These truths are the post-resurrection pattern for the daily practice of Christ's own words: "Abide in me, and I in you. As the branch cannot bear fruit of itself, except it abide in the vine; no more can ye, except ye abide in me" (John 15:4). Great are the resources of the Christian life. "If any man be in Christ, he is a new creature: old things are passed away; behold, all things are become new" (II Cor. 5:17). The resurrection guarantees the untarnishable reality of this shining truth.

After the death of Robert Schumann, his wife, a great pianist in her own right, devoted herself to making her husband's works known. Along with hours of disciplined practice before her concerts, she prepared for the interpretation of the music by reading again the treasured letters the great composer had written her. But Christians have far more than the letters of a dead man. They have the inspired Word of the living Lord, the Book of which he said, "Search the scriptures; for... they are they which testify of me" (John 5:39). Not only so, but Christians also have within them the Spirit of their risen Saviour. And theirs is the obligation to live and walk with him in the discipline of daily life.

In his *Aims of Education,* Alfred North Whitehead distinguishes between "inert" ideas and ideas that are alive and effective. Held only as a doctrinal fact or accepted merely as a beautiful vision, the resurrection may be nothing more than "inert" knowledge. But God means it to be otherwise. He appoints Christians today, as in every age, to be witnesses of this event that happened in the first century. He means them to know its continuing power through a committed life, and he means them to speak not from hearsay, but out of personal experience of the risen Lord.

— *Christianity Today*, March 27, 1964

Thirty
CHRIST COMES TWICE

The Advent season relates to a future certainty as well as to a past event. It looks back to the stupendous miracle of the incarnation of him who is the light of the world, inextinguishable amid all the darkness of human failure and sin. But it also looks forward to the return of this same Jesus, who was born in Bethlehem that he might die and be raised to save us from our sins and give us life everlasting. For just as the Bible tells of his First Coming, so it promises his Second Coming.

In the Book of Common Prayer, this Collect with its recognition of the two Comings is used throughout Advent: "Almighty God, give us grace that we may cast away the works of darkness, and put upon us the armour of light, now in the time of this mortal life, in which thy Son Jesus Christ came to visit us in great humility; that in the last day, when he shall come again in his glorious majesty to judge both the quick and the dead, we may rise to the life immortal, through him who liveth and reigneth with thee and the Holy Ghost, now and ever. Amen."

To forget the Second Advent, as many do, or, while acknowledging it, to dissipate its reality by spiritualizing the plain promises of his coming or by adopting some extreme kind of "realized eschatology," is to be deprived of what the New Testament calls "the blessed [literally, 'happy'] hope." The deprivation is serious, especially in this apocalyptic age when Christians so greatly need the assurance of the ultimate triumph of Jesus Christ. Yet honesty requires the admission that there are many who, while holding orthodox views of the Second Advent, do not really know it as the comfort and incentive it should be for every Christian. Granted that there are diverse interpretations of the Scriptures dealing with the Lord's return — and such differences ought never to hinder Christian fellowship — still there are few doctrines about which there is more widespread ignorance than this one.

While some have fallen into such unbiblical errors as setting the date of his coming and while certain cults have distorted the doctrine of the Second Advent almost beyond recognition, it is well to remember that the misuse of a truth never invalidates that truth. Nor is this the only doctrine that has been distorted; church history records countless heresies about other great truths of the faith. To lose one's grip on "the promise of his coming" or to be disinterested in it is to miss one of the great biblical sources of comfort, hope, and urgency for service.

Some years ago Bertrand Russell wrote an essay for *The Atlantic Monthly* (March, 1951) on the future of mankind. In it he predicted that before this century ends, "unless something unforeseeable occurs, one of three possibilities will have been realized . . . 1. The end of human life, perhaps of all life on our planet. 2. A reversion to barbarism after a catastrophic diminution of the population of the globe. 3. A unification of the world under a single government. . . ." But what for Earl Russell is "something unforeseeable" is a certainty for the Christian who believes in the Second Coming.

The ultimate key to human history is not in the hands of men with their nuclear weapons but in the pierced hands of the Prince of Peace. For the man of the world, Christ is indeed the unknown and unforeseeable factor. But everyone who believes the promises spoken by our Lord and the teaching of the prophets and the apostles should know that history is not circular but that with Jesus Christ crucified and risen as its midpoint it is moving on to the Parousia and the culmination of all things in him. He knows on the authority of the Word that the same Lord who saved him is coming back, that in his presence there will be the inexpressible comfort of reunion with those who "sleep in Jesus," that he must stand before the judgment seat of Christ, that this whole world order is to be judged, that Christ who is King of kings and Lord of lords will defeat Satan, and that in Christ the Kingdom will be fully realized. Differences of interpretation in these things, yes; but about the fact that history will come to its close in and through Christ there is no biblical ground for disagreement.

The Second Advent with its teaching of the end of this world order is repugnant to the modern mind. If, as C. S. Lewis put it in *The World's Last Night,* we live under the possibility that "the curtain may be rung down at any moment" on human history, then the pride of man is indeed shattered. But in a time when the destructive capacity of man has so dangerously outrun his moral control and when the prospect of lunar voyages and interplanetary travel contributes to the arrogant self-confidence of a generation that cannot live peacefully on this planet, the Second Advent has much to say. A society that, like those in the Lord's parable, "will not have this man to reign over us," and that as a consequence of this rejection is casting aside all moral restraints, almost inevitably falls into the Promethean spirit of challenging the Almighty himself. Even now what Communism is saying about the Lord and his Anointed sounds like a paraphrase of these words from the Second Psalm: "Let us break their bands asunder and cast their cords from us." And let us remember that the secularism prevading our nation is little more than an indirect form of the same denial of God and his Christ.

Whenever a great doctrine of Scripture is overlooked or ignored, the Church suffers and its witness is weakened. Ours is a society that needs to hear not only the good news of the First Advent but also the certainty of the Second Advent. It needs to know that Scripture gives no assurance that God will put up with human sin and rebellion forever. It is part of the obligation of the Church to tell men and women that God has a plan for the world and that this plan culminates in Christ. Moreover, Christians themselves need to be taught the truth of their Lord's return, because believing it leads to purity of life. As the beloved disciple said, "We know that when he appears we shall be like him, for we shall see him as he is. And every one who thus hopes in him purifies himself as he is pure" (I John 3:2, 3, RSV). Not only so, but as our Lord said in the parable of the talent and in other of his teachings, the expectation of his coming brings urgency to service. Over and over he declared that he will come back. The time of his return is unknown, although the fact is sure. And today, as never before, "the fields are white unto the harvest." Therein lies the urgency of the Second Advent. Very much remains to be done for him who is coming.

When Britain was about to grant independence to India, the viceroy, Lord Mountbatten, had a certain kind of calendar printed. One of the news photographs made in his office showed the wall calendar, which read at the time when the picture was taken: "4 August. 11 days left to prepare for transfer of power." In this way the viceroy reminded himself and the other servants of the crown of the coming transfer of power, when the sub-continent would pass from British to national rule. But the world is waiting for a vastly greater transfer of power, when the Son whose right it is to reign shall come and take the power and reign forever and ever.

No human calendar marks the time until he comes; only he with whom "one day is as a thousand years and a thousand years as one day" knows the day and the hour when the Son of man will return. But in the meantime there is work to be done in the name of Christ, there is the Gospel that is "a savour of life unto life and death unto death" to be proclaimed, there is life to be lived in accord with the will of the Lord and to his glory — and there is all this to be done in the expectation of his coming. Two Advents, and the second demands proclamation as well as the first!

Christianity Today, December 20, 1963